Declarative Networking

Synthesis Lectures on Data Management

Editor
M. Tamer Özsu, *University of Waterloo*

Synthesis Lectures on Data Management is edited by Tamer Özsu of the University of Waterloo. The series will publish 50- to 125 page publications on topics pertaining to data management. The scope will largely follow the purview of premier information and computer science conferences, such as ACM SIGMOD, VLDB, ICDE, PODS, ICDT, and ACM KDD. Potential topics include, but not are limited to: query languages, database system architectures, transaction management, data warehousing, XML and databases, data stream systems, wide scale data distribution, multimedia data management, data mining, and related subjects.

Declarative Networking
Boon Thau Loo and Wenchao Zhou
2012

Full-Text (Substring) Indexes in External Memory
Marina Barsky, Ulrike Stege, and Alex Thomo
2011

Spatial Data Management
Nikos Mamoulis
2011

Database Repairing and Consistent Query Answering
Leopoldo Bertossi
2011

Managing Event Information: Modeling, Retrieval, and Applications
Amarnath Gupta and Ramesh Jain
2011

Fundamentals of Physical Design and Query Compilation
David Toman and Grant Weddell
2011

User-Centered Data Management
Tiziana Catarci, Alan Dix, Stephen Kimani, and Giuseppe Santucci
2010

Data Stream Management
Lukasz Golab and M. Tamer Özsu
2010

Access Control in Data Management Systems
Elena Ferrari
2010

An Introduction to Duplicate Detection
Felix Naumann and Melanie Herschel
2010

Privacy-Preserving Data Publishing: An Overview
Raymond Chi-Wing Wong and Ada Wai-Chee Fu
2010

Keyword Search in Databases
Jeffrey Xu Yu, Lu Qin, and Lijun Chang
2009

Declarative Networking

Boon Thau Loo and Wenchao Zhou

ISBN: 978-3-031-00758-3   paperback
ISBN: 978-3-031-01886-2   ebook

DOI 10.1007/978-3-031-01886-2

A Publication in the Springer series
SYNTHESIS LECTURES ON DATA MANAGEMENT

Lecture #23
Series Editor: M. Tamer Özsu, *University of Waterloo*
Series ISSN
Synthesis Lectures on Data Management
Print 2153-5418   Electronic 2153-5426

Declarative Networking

Boon Thau Loo and Wenchao Zhou
University of Pennsylvania

SYNTHESIS LECTURES ON DATA MANAGEMENT #23

ABSTRACT

Declarative Networking is a programming methodology that enables developers to concisely specify network protocols and services, which are directly compiled to a dataflow framework that executes the specifications. Declarative networking proposes the use of a declarative query language for specifying and implementing network protocols, and employs a dataflow framework at runtime for communication and maintenance of network state. The primary goal of declarative networking is to greatly simplify the process of specifying, implementing, deploying and evolving a network design. In addition, declarative networking serves as an important step towards an extensible, evolvable network architecture that can support *flexible*, *secure* and *efficient* deployment of new network protocols.

This book provides an introduction to basic issues in declarative networking, including language design, optimization and dataflow execution. The methodology behind declarative programming of networks is presented, including roots in Datalog, extensions for networked environments, and the semantics of long-running queries over network state. The book focuses on a representative declarative networking language called *Network Datalog* (NDlog), which is based on extensions to the Datalog recursive query language. An overview of declarative network protocols written in NDlog is provided, and its usage is illustrated using examples from routing protocols and overlay networks.

This book also describes the implementation of a declarative networking engine and NDlog execution strategies that provide eventual consistency semantics with significant flexibility in execution. Two representative declarative networking systems (P2 and its successor RapidNet) are presented. Finally, the book highlights recent advances in declarative networking, and new declarative approaches to related problems.

KEYWORDS

declarative networking, datalog, recursive query processing

To Foo Lee Yoong

(Boon Thau Loo's mother)

and

To Yiqing Ren

(Wenchao Zhou's wife)

February 2012.

Contents

Acknowledgments

The technical contents from Chapter 1-7 are derived from Boon Thau Loo's doctoral dissertation [Loo, 2006] (advisors: Joseph M. Hellerstein and Ion Stoica, with significant input from Raghu Ramakrishnan), and collectively contributed by members of the P2 declarative networking team [P2] at the University of California Berkeley, and Intel Labs. Declarative networking research at the University of California Berkeley was funded by NSF grants (IIS-0205647, IIS-0209108, and ANI-0225660) and a gift from Microsoft.

At the University of Pennsylvania, our work on declarative networking has been funded by NSF (CNS-0721845, CNS-0831376, IIS-0812270, CCF-0820208, CNS-0845552, CNS-1040672, CNS-1065130, and CNS-1117052), AFOSR MURI grant FA9550-08-1-0352, DARPA SAFER award N66001-11-C-4020, and DARPA Air Force Research Laboratory (AFRL) Contract FA8750-07-C-0169. We thank our collaborators listed on the NetDB@Penn site [NetDB@Penn] for their contributions to the various research efforts described in this book, in particular, Chapter 8.

Finally, we thank Tamer Özsu for his useful comments and input into this book. We also thank Harjot Gill, Alex Gurney, Anduo Wang, and Zhuoyao Zhang for their careful proofreading of this book.

Boon Thau Loo and Wenchao Zhou
February 2012

Figure Credits

Figure 3.4   *is from* Shivkumar C. Muthukumar, Xiaozhou Li, Changbin Liu, Joseph B. Kopena, Mihai Oprea, Ricardo Correa, Boon Thau Loo, and Prithwish Basu. RapidMesh: declarative toolkit for rapid experimentation of wireless mesh networks. In *Proc. ACM Int. Workshop on Wireless Network Testbeds, Experimental Evaluation and Characterization*, pages 1–10, 2009a. Copyright © 2009 ACM. Used with permission. And Shivkumar C. Muthukumar, Xiaozhou Li, Changbin Liu, Joseph B. Kopena, Mihai Oprea, and Boon Thau Loo. Declarative toolkit for rapid network protocol simulation and experimentation. In *Proc. ACM Int. Conf. on Data Communication*, pages 1–2, 2009b. Copyright © 2009 ACM. Used with permission.

Figure 8.4   *is from* Wenchao Zhou, Qiong Fei, Shengzhi Sun, Tao Tao, Andreas Haeberlen, Zachary Ives, Boon Thau Loo, and Micah Sherr. NetTrails: A Declarative Platform for Provenance Maintenance and Querying in Distributed Systems. In *Proc. ACM SIGMOD Int. Conf. on Management of Data*, pages 1323–1326, 2011c. Copyright ©2011 ACM. Used with permission.

CHAPTER 1

Introduction

Over the past decade, there has been intense interest in the design of new network protocols. This has been driven from below by an increasing diversity in network architectures (including wireless networks, satellite communications, and delay-tolerant rural networks) and from above by a quickly growing suite of networked applications (peer-to-peer systems, sensor networks, content distribution, etc.)

Network protocol design and implementation is a challenging process. This is not only because of the distributed nature and large scale of typical networks, but also because of the need to balance the extensibility and flexibility of these protocols on one hand, and their robustness and efficiency on the other hand. One need look no further than the Internet for an illustration of these hard tradeoffs. Today's Internet routing protocols, while arguably robust and efficient, make it hard to accommodate the needs of new applications such as improved resilience and higher throughput. Upgrading even a single router is hard. Getting a distributed routing protocol implemented correctly is even harder. And, in order to change or upgrade a deployed routing protocol today, one must get access to *each* router to modify its software. This process is made even more tedious and error-prone by the use of conventional programming languages.

This book presents the design and implementation of *declarative networking* [Loo et al., 2005a,b, 2006, 2009], an application of database query-language and processing techniques to the domain of networking. Declarative networking is based on the observation that network protocols deal at their core with computing and maintaining distributed state (e.g., routes, sessions, performance statistics) according to basic information locally available at each node (e.g., neighbor tables, link measurements, local clocks) while enforcing constraints such as local routing policies. Recursive query languages studied in the deductive database literature [Ramakrishnan and Ullman, 1993] are a natural fit for expressing the relationship between base data, derived data, and the associated constraints. Simple extensions to these languages and their implementations enable the natural expression and efficient execution of network protocols.

The high-level goal of declarative networking is to provide software environments that can accelerate the process of specifying, implementing, experimenting with and evolving designs for network architectures. Declarative networking can reduce program sizes by orders of magnitude relative to traditional approaches, in some cases resulting in programs that are line-for-line translations of pseudocode in networking research papers. In addition to serving as a platform for rapid prototyping of network protocols, declarative networking also open up opportunities for automatic protocol optimization and hybridization, program checking and debugging.

As evidence of its widespread applicability, declarative techniques have been used in several domains including fault tolerance protocols [Singh et al., 2008], cloud computing [Alvaro et al., 2010], sensor networks [Chu et al., 2007], overlay network compositions [Mao et al., 2008], anonymity systems [Sherr et al., 2010], mobile ad-hoc networks [Liu et al., 2011a, Muthukumar et al., 2009a], wireless channel selection [Liu et al., 2012], network configuration management [Chen et al., 2010], and as a basis for course projects in a distributed systems class [Gill et al., 2011] at the University of Pennsylvania. An open-source declarative networking platform called *Rapid-Net* [RapidNet] has also been integrated with the emerging ns-3 [ns-3] simulator, demonstrated at SIGCOMM'09 [Muthukumar et al., 2009b], and successfully deployed on testbeds such as Planet-Lab [PlanetLab] and ORBIT [ORBIT].

1.1 OVERVIEW OF DECLARATIVE NETWORKS

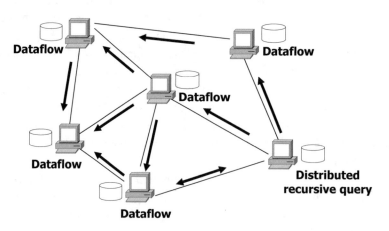

Figure 1.1: A Declarative Network

Figure 1.1 illustrates a declarative network at a conceptual level. Like any traditional network, a declarative network maintains network state at each node to enable the routing and forwarding of packets. The network state is stored as relational tables distributed across the network, similar to a traditional distributed database [Özsu and Valduriez, 2011]. Network protocols are declaratively specified as distributed recursive queries over the network state. Recursive queries have traditionally been used in the database community for posing queries over graph structures in deductive databases. The main observation that inspired this work on declarative networking is that these recursive queries are a natural fit for expressing network protocols, which themselves are based on recursive relations among nodes in the network.

The recursive query language used in declarative networking is a distributed variant of Datalog called *Network Datalog (NDlog)*. Intuitively, one can view the forwarding tables generated by network protocols as the output of distributed recursive queries over changing input network state (network links, nodes, load, operator policies, etc.), and the query results need to be kept consistent at all times with the changing network state.

Network protocols are specified as NDlog programs and disseminated in the network. Upon receiving NDlog programs, each node compiles the declarative specifications into execution plans in the form of distributed dataflows. When executed, these dataflows generate message exchanges among nodes as well as network state modifications, resulting in the implementation of the network protocols. Multiple declarative networks can run simultaneously, either as separate dataflows, or compiled into a single dataflow where common functionalities among the protocols can be shared.

1.2   THE CASE FOR DECLARATIVE NETWORKING

Declarative networking presents three advantages over existing approaches: *ease of programming*, *optimizability* and *balance between extensibility and safety*. We summarize the advantages in the rest of this section.

1.2.1   EASE OF PROGRAMMING

A declarative language allows us to specify at a high level "what" to do, rather than "how" to do it. When feasible, the declarative approach can lead to ease of programming and significant reduction in code size. As demonstrated in Chapter 5, NDlog can express a variety of well-known routing protocols (e.g., distance vector, path vector, dynamic source routing, link state, multicast) in a compact and clean fashion, typically in a handful of lines of program code. Moreover, higher-level routing concepts (e.g., QoS constraints) can be achieved via simple modifications to these programs. Furthermore, Chapter 6 shows that complex application-level overlay networks can also be expressed naturally in NDlog.

Declarative network descriptions can be extremely concise. For example, the Chord overlay network can be specified in 48 NDlog rules, versus thousands of lines of code for the MIT Chord reference implementation. Also, the high-level, declarative specifications means that they decompose cleanly into logically reusable units: for instance, for composing various overlay networks together [Mao et al., 2008]. Moreover, by providing a uniform declarative language for distributed querying and networking, we enable the natural integration of distributed information-gathering tasks like resource discovery and network status monitoring.

In addition to ease of programming, there are other advantages to the use of a high level language. For example, NDlog specifications can illustrate unexpected relations between network protocols, as we illustrate in Chapter 7. In particular, the path vector and dynamic source routing protocols differ only in a simple, traditional database optimization decision: the order in which a query's predicates are evaluated. The use of higher-level abstractions also provides the potential to statically check network protocols for security and correctness properties. Dynamic runtime checks to test distributed properties of the network can also be easily expressed as declarative queries, providing a uniform framework for network specification, monitoring and debugging.

1.2.2   OPTIMIZABILITY

Declarative networking achieves performance comparable to traditional approaches. Moreover, by using a declarative framework rooted in databases, better performance can be achieved by utilizing query processing and optimization techniques that are well-studied in the database community.

The declarative approach to protocol specification reveals new opportunities for optimizing network protocols. First, the use of a high-level declarative language facilitates the identification and sharing of common functionalities among different declarative networks. Second, off-the-shelf database optimization techniques can be applied to declarative routing specifications to achieve tangible performance benefits. Third, new optimization techniques suited to the distributed, soft-state context of network protocols are developed.

1.2.3   BALANCE OF EXTENSIBILITY AND SAFETY

In addition to the benefits of having a higher-level, compact specification, declarative networking achieves a better balance between *extensibility* and *safety* compared to existing solutions. Extensibility, or the ability to easily add new functionality to existing systems, is an important requirement in our setting as a means of rapid deployment and experimentation with network protocols. However, extensibility has traditionally been achieved at the expense of security [Bershad et al., 1995, Stonebraker, 1986]. In the network domain, this concern is best illustrated by active networks [Tennenhouse et al., 1997] which, at the extreme, allow routers to download and execute arbitrary code. While active networks provide full generality, security concerns have limited their practical use.

Declarative networking can be viewed as a safer, restricted instantiation of active networks, where NDlog is proposed as a Domain Specific Language (DSL) for programming a network. The core of NDlog is Datalog, which has complexity polynomial in the size of the network state [Abiteboul et al., 1995]. While the language extensions to NDlog alter its theoretical worst-case complexity, there exist static analysis tests on termination for a large class of recursive queries [Krishnamurthy et al., 1996]. This addresses the *safety* aspect of security, where specified protocols can now be checked to ensure that they do not consume infinite resources before execution. In addition, by "sandboxing" NDlog programs within a database query engine, undesirable side-effects are contained during query execution. Safety analysis of declarative networking protocols will be discussed in Chapter 8.

1.3   ORGANIZATION

This book is organized as follows.

Chapter 2 provides an introduction to Datalog, and then motivates and formally defines the NDlog language. NDlog builds upon traditional Datalog to enable *distributed* and *soft-state* computations based on the underlying physical connectivity, all of which are essential in the network setting.

Chapter 3 describes the implementation of a declarative networking engine, and query processing techniques for compiling NDlog programs into execution plans. We further introduce two representative open-source declarative networking engines, P2 [P2] and its successor *Rapid-Net* [RapidNet].

Chapter 4 introduces relaxed versions of the traditional, centralized execution strategy known as *semi-naïve* [Balbin and Ramamohanarao, 1987] fixpoint evaluation. The *pipelined semi-naïve* evaluation technique overcome fundamental problems of semi-naïve evaluation in an asynchronous distributed setting. In the network setting, transactional isolation of updates from concurrent queries is often inappropriate; network protocols must incorporate concurrent updates about the state of the network while they run. This is addressed by formalizing the typical distributed systems notion of "eventual consistency" in declarative networking's context of derived data. Using techniques from materialized recursive view maintenance, updates to input tables during NDlog program execution are incorporated, while ensuring well-defined eventual consistency semantics.

Chapter 5 demonstrates the expressiveness of NDlog in compactly specifying declarative routing protocols that implement a variety of well-known routing protocols. NDlog programs are a natural and compact way of expressing a variety of well-known routing protocols, typically in a handful of lines of program code. This allows ease of customization, where higher-level routing concepts (e.g., QoS constraints) can be achieved via simple modifications to the NDlog programs.

Chapter 6 further applies the declarative framework to more challenging scenarios, where NDlog is used to specify complex overlay networks such as the Narada mesh [Chu et al., 2000] for end-system multicast and the Chord distributed hash table. The declarative Chord implementation is roughly two orders of magnitude less code than the original C++ implementation.

Chapter 7 discusses and evaluates a number of query optimizations that arise in the declarative networking context. These include applications of traditional database techniques such as aggregate selections [Furfaro et al., 2002, Sudarshan and Ramakrishnan, 1991] and magic-sets rewriting [Bancilhon et al., 1986, Beeri and Ramakrishnan, 1987], as well as new optimizations we develop for work-sharing, caching, and cost-based optimizations based on graph statistics.

Chapter 8 describes recent advances in declarative networking, tracing its evolution from a rapid prototyping framework towards a platform that serves as an important bridge connecting formal theories for reasoning about protocol correctness and actual implementations. In particular, the chapter presents recent uses of declarative networking for addressing four main challenges in the distributed systems development cycle: the generation of safe routing implementations, debugging, security and privacy, and optimizing distributed systems.

Chapter 9 concludes by summarizing the overall impact of declarative networking.

CHAPTER 2

Declarative Networking Language

This chapter formally defines the Network Datalog (NDlog) language for declarative networking. The NDlog language is based on extensions to traditional Datalog, a well-known recursive query language designed and traditionally used for querying graph-structured data in a centralized database.

This chapter is organized as follows. Section 2.1 provides an introduction to Datalog. Section 2.2 presents the NDlog language using an example program that computes all-pairs shortest paths in a network from specification to execution. Based on this example program, NDlog extensions to traditional Datalog are highlighted. Furthermore, the connection to routing is established, by showing that the execution of this program resembles a well-known routing protocol for computing shortest paths in a network.

Following the example, in Sections 2.3, 2.4 and 2.5, we formally describe the data and query model of NDlog that addresses its four main requirements: *distributed computation, soft-state data and rules*, and *incremental maintenance of network state*.

2.1 INTRODUCTION TO DATALOG

Following the conventions in the Ramakrishnan and Ullman [1993] survey, a Datalog program consists of a set of declarative *rules* and an optional *query*. Since these programs are commonly called *"recursive queries"* in the database literature, the terms "query" and "program" are used interchangeably when referring to a Datalog program.

A Datalog *rule* has the form $p : - q_1, q_2, ..., q_n.$, which can be read informally as "q_1 and q_2 and ... and q_n imply p". The predicate p is the *head* of the rule, and $q_1, q_2, ..., q_n$ is a list of *literals* that constitutes the *body* of the rule. Literals are either *predicates* over *fields* (variables and constants), or function symbols applied to fields. The rules can refer to each other in a cyclic fashion to express recursion. The order in which the rules are presented in a program is semantically immaterial. The commas separating the predicates in a rule are logical conjuncts (*AND*); the order in which predicates appear in a rule body also has no semantic significance, though most implementations (including declarative networking engines) employ a left-to-right execution strategy. The *query* specifies the output of interest.

The predicates in the body and head of traditional Datalog rules are relations, and they are interchangeably referred to in this book as predicates, relations or tables. The number and types of fields in relations are inferred from their (consistent) use in the program's rules. Each relation has a *primary key*, which consists of a set of fields that uniquely identify each tuple within the relation. In the absence of other information, the primary key is taken to be the full set of fields in the relation.

By convention, the names of predicates, function symbols and constants begin with a lower-case letter, while variable names begin with an upper-case letter. Most implementations of Datalog enhance it with a limited set of function calls (which start with "f_" in NDlog's syntax), including boolean predicates and arithmetic computations. Aggregate constructs are represented as functions with field variables within angle brackets (<>). Negated predicates are not used in declarative networking.

As an example, Figure 2.1 shows a Datalog program that computes the next hop along the shortest paths between all pairs of nodes in a graph. The program abbreviates some of its predicates as shown in Figure 2.2. The program has four rules (which for convenience are labeled r1-r4), and takes as input a base ("extensional") relation link(Source, Destination, Cost). Rules r1-r2 are used to derive "paths" in the graph, represented as tuples in the derived ("intensional") relation path(S,D,Z,C). The S and D fields represent the source and destination endpoints of the path; Z contains the "next hop" in the graph along the path that a node S should take in order to go to node D; and C represents the cost of the path.

Rule r1 produces path tuples directly from existing link tuples, and rule r2 recursively produces path tuples of increasing cost by matching (or *unifying*) the destination fields of existing links to the source fields of previously computed paths. The matching is expressed using the repeated "Z" variable in link(S,Z,C1) and path(Z,D,Z2,C2) of rule r2. Intuitively, rule r2 says that "if there is a link from node S to node Z, and there is a path from node Z to node D, then there is a path from node S to node D via Z".

Given the path relation, rule r3 derives the relation spCost(S,D,C) that computes the minimum cost C for each source (S) and destination (D) for all input paths. Rule r4 takes as input spCost and path tuples and then computes shortestPathHop(S,D,Z,C) tuples that contains the next hop (Z) along the shortest path from S to D with cost C. Last, the *Query* specifies the output of interest to be the shortestPath table.

---

r1 path(S,D,D,C) :- link(S,D,C).
r2 path(S,D,Z,C) :- link(S,Z,C1), path(Z,D,Z2,C2), C = C1 + C2.
r3 spCost(S,D,min<C>) :- path(S,D,Z,C).
r4 shortestPathHop(S,D,C) :- spCost(S,D,C), path(S,D,Z,C).
Query shortestPathHop(S,D,Z,C).

Figure 2.1: Shortest-Path-Hop Datalog program.

2.2 NETWORK DATALOG BY EXAMPLE

Before diving into the formal definitions of NDlog, Figure 2.3 shows an example using a distributed variant of the earlier *Shortest-Path-Hop* Datalog program. This distributed NDlog program computes

Predicate	Schema
link(S,D,C)	path(Source,Destination,Cost)
path(S,D,Z,C)	path(Source,Destination,NextHop,Cost)
spCost(S,D,C)	spCost(Source,Destination,Cost)
shortestPathHop(S,D,Z,C)	shortestPathHop(Source,Destination,NextHop,Cost)

Figure 2.2: Predicates and the corresponding schemas used in the *Shortest-Path-Hop* Datalog program shown in Figure 2.1.

```
materialize(link,infinity,infinity,keys(1,2)).
materialize(path,infinity,infinity,keys(1,2,3,4)).
materialize(spCost,infinity,infinity,keys(1,2)).
materialize(shortestPathHop,infinity,infinity,keys(1,2)).
sh1 path(@S,D,D,C) :- link(@S,D,C).
sh2 path(@S,D,Z,C) :- link(@S,Z,C1), path(@Z,D,Z2,C2), C = C1 + C2.
sh3 spCost(@S,D,min<C>) :- path(@S,D,Z,C).
sh4 shortestPathHop(@S,D,Z,C) :- spCost(@S,D,C), path(@S,D,Z,C).
Query shortestPathHop(@S,D,Z,C).
```

Figure 2.3: Shortest-Path-Hop NDlog program.

for every node, the next hop along the shortest paths of all nodes in a network in a distributed fashion. This NDlog program is used to highlight the following key points:

- NDlog builds upon traditional Datalog in order to meet three new requirements: *distributed computation*, *soft-state data and rules*, and *incremental maintenance of network state*.

- When this program is executed, the resulting communication and network state resembles the well-known *distance vector* and *path vector* routing protocols [Peterson and Davie, 2007].

- This example program demonstrates the compactness of NDlog. In four NDlog rules, one can specify and implement a routing protocol widely used to compute shortest routes in a network.

2.2.1   OVERVIEW OF NDLOG

An NDlog program is largely composed of table declaration statements and rules. In NDlog, all input relations and rule derivations are stored in *materialized* tables. Unlike Datalog, tables must be defined explicitly in NDlog via `materialize` statements, which specify constraints on the size and lifetime of tuple storage—any relations not declared as tables are treated as named *streams* of tuples. Each `materialize(name, lifetime, size, primary keys)` statement specifies the relation name, lifetime of each tuple in the relation, maximum size of the relation, and fields making up the primary key of each relation[1]. If the primary key is the empty set (), then the primary key is the full set of fields in the relation. For example, in the *Shortest-Path-Hop* NDlog program, all the tables are specified with infinite sizes and lifetimes.

The execution of NDlog rules will result in the derivation of tuples that are stored in materialized tables. For the duration of program execution, these materialized results are incrementally recomputed as the input relations are updated. For example, the update of `link` tuples will result in new derivations and updates to existing `path`, `spCost` and `shortestPathHop` tuples. In addition, if an NDlog rule head is prepended with an optional keyword *delete*, the derived tuples are used to delete an exact match tuple in its relation instead.

Since network protocols are typically computations over distributed network state, one of the important requirements of NDlog is the ability to support rules that express distributed computations. NDlog builds upon traditional Datalog by providing control over the storage location of tuples explicitly in the syntax via *location specifiers*. Each location specifier is an attribute within a predicate that indicates the partitioning field of each relation. To illustrate, in Figure 2.3, each predicate in the NDlog rules has an "@" symbol prepended to a single field denoting the location specifier. For example, all `path` and `link` tuples are stored based on the address stored in the first field @S.

Interestingly, while NDlog is a language to describe networks, there are no explicit communication primitives. All communication is implicitly generated during rule execution as a result of data placement. For example, in rule `sh2`, the `path` and `link` predicates have different location specifiers, and in order to execute the rule body of `sh2` based on their matching fields, `link` and `path` tuples have to be shipped in the network. It is the movement of these tuples that will generate the messages for the resulting network protocol.

2.2.2   FROM QUERY SPECIFICATIONS TO PROTOCOL EXECUTION

Having provided a high-level overview of NDlog, the execution of the *Shortest-Path-Hop* NDlog program is demonstrated via an example network shown in Figure 2.4. The resulting communication and network state generated in program execution resembles the distance-vector protocol [Peterson and Davie, 2007] that is commonly used to compute shortest paths in a network.

In the example network, each node is running the *Shortest-Path-Hop* program. For simplicity, only the derived paths along the solid lines are shown, even though the network connectivity is bidirectional (dashed lines). The discussion is necessarily informal since distributed implementation strategies have not yet been presented. Chapter 4 shows in greater detail the steps required to generate the execution plan. Here, the focus is on providing a high-level understanding of the data movement in the network during query processing.

In this example, communication is simplified and described in *iterations*, where at each iteration, each network node generates `paths` of increasing hop count, and then propagates these paths to neighbor nodes along links. Each `path` tuple contains the `nextHop` field, which indicates for

---

[1]The convention used in declarative networking starts the offset by 1 in the declarative networking system, as 0 is reserved in the implementation for the table name.

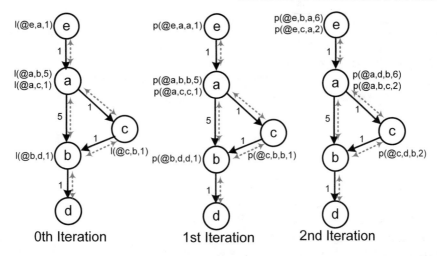

Figure 2.4: Shortest-Path program example execution. l and p are used as abbreviations for link and path respectively.

each path the next hop to route the message in the network. In Figure 2.4, we show newly derived path tuples at each iteration. In the first iteration, all nodes initialize their local path tables to 1-hop path tuples using rule sh1. In the 2nd iteration, using rule sh2, each node takes the input path tuples generated in the previous iteration, and computes 2-hop paths, which are then propagated to its neighbors. For example, path(@a,d,b,6) is generated at node b using path(@b,d,d,1) from the second iteration, and propagated to node a.

As path tuples are being computed and received at nodes, spCost and shortestPathHop tuples are also incrementally computed. For example, node a computes path(@a,b,b,5) using rule sh1, and then derives spCost(@a,b,5) and shortestPathHop(@a,b,b,5) using rules sh4-sh5. In the next iteration, node a receives path(@a,b,c,2) from node c which has lower cost compared to the previous shortest cost of 5, and hence the new tuples spCost(@a,b,2) and shortestPathHop(@a,b,c,2) replaces the previous values.

In the presence of path cycles, the *Shortest-Path-Hop* program never terminates, as rules sp1 and sp2 will generate paths of ever increasing costs. However, this can be fixed by storing the entire path and adding a check for cycles within the rules. Alternatively, a well-known optimization (Section 7.1.1) can be used when costs are positive to avoid cycles. Intuitively, this optimization reduces communication overhead by sending only the path tuples that result in changes to the local spCost and shortestPathHop tables, hence limiting communication to only path tuples that contribute to the eventual shortest paths.

Interestingly, the computation of the above program resembles the computation of the distance vector protocol. In the distance vector protocol, each node advertises <destination, path-cost> information to all neighbors, which is similar to the path tuples exchanged by

---

Algorithm 2.1 Pseudocode for the *Shortest-Path-Hop* NDlog program

---

$path(@Z, D, D, C) \leftarrow link(@Z, D, C)$ [Rule sh1]

while receive $< path(@Z, D, Z2, C2) >$

    for each neighbor $link(@S, D, C)$ [Rule sh2]

        send $path(@S, D, Z, C1 + C2)$ **to** neighbor @S

    end

end

```
materialize(link,infinity,infinity,keys(1,2)).
materialize(path,infinity,infinity,keys(4)).
materialize(spCost,infinity,infinity,keys(1,2)).
materialize(shortestPath,infinity,infinity,keys(1,2)).
sp1 path(@S,D,D,P,C) :- link(@S,D,C), P = f_init(S,D).
sp2 path(@S,D,Z,P,C) :- link(@S,Z,C1), path(@Z,D,Z2,P2,C2), C = C1 + C2,
                        P = f_concatPath(S,P2).
sp3 spCost(@S,D,min<C>) :- path(@S,D,Z,P,C).
sp4 shortestPath(@S,D,P,C) :- spCost(@S,D,C), path(@S,D,Z,P,C).
Query shortestPath(@S,D,P,C).
```

Figure 2.5: Shortest-Path NDlog program.

nodes at each iteration. All nodes use these advertisements to update their routing tables with the next hop along the shortest paths for each given destination. This is similar to computing new `shortestPathHop` tuples from `path` tuples using rules sh3–sh4. The main difference between the NDlog program and the actual distance vector computation is that rather than sending individual path tuples between neighbors, the traditional distance vector method batches together a vector of costs for all neighbors.

In the *Shortest-Path-Hop* program, the protocol only propagates the *nextHop* and not the entire path. In most practical network protocols such as the Border Gateway Protocol (BGP) [Peterson and Davie, 2007], the entire path is included either for source routing or more commonly, to prevent infinite path cycles. This is typically known as the *path vector* protocol, where the *path vector* is the list of nodes from the source to the destination.

Figure 2.5 shows the *Shortest-Path* NDlog program that implements the path-vector protocol. The program is written with only minor modifications to the earlier *Shortest-Path-Hop* NDlog program. The program computes the entire path for a given source to destination, by adding an extra field in the `path` predicate that maintains the full path. The function `f_init(X,Y)` initializes the path with nodes X and Y, and the function `f_concatPath(N,P)` prepends a node N to an existing path P. Chapter 5 presents more examples of routing protocols.

2.2.3   OTHER REQUIREMENTS OF NDLOG

In addition to distributed computations, NDlog requires the following additional features for *soft-state data and rules* and *incremental maintenance of network state*. These features are briefly described here, followed by more detailed descriptions in the rest of the book.

- **Soft-state data and rules:** In typical network protocols, the generated network state is maintained as *soft-state* [Clark, 1988] data. In the soft-state storage model, stored data have a *lifetime* or time-to-live (TTL), and are deleted when the lifetime has expired. The soft-state storage model requires periodic communication to refresh network state. Soft-state is often favored in networking implementations because in a very simple manner it provides well-defined eventual consistency semantics. Intuitively, periodic refreshes to network state ensure that the eventual values are obtained even if there are transient errors such as reordered messages, node disconnection or link failures. While soft-state is useful for maintaining distributed state, declarative networking also makes extensive use of traditional *"hard-state"* data with infinite lifetimes for storing persistent counters, local machine state and archival logs.

- **Incremental maintenance of network state:** In practice, most network protocols are executed over a long period of time, and the protocol incrementally updates and repairs routing tables as the underlying network changes (link failures, node departures, etc). To better map into practical networking scenarios, one key distinction that differentiates the execution of NDlog from earlier work in Datalog is the support for continuous rule execution and results materialization, where all tuples derived from NDlog rules are materialized and incrementally updated as the underlying network changes. As in network protocols, such incremental maintenance is required both for timely updates and for avoiding the overhead of recomputing all routing tables "from scratch" whenever there are changes to the underlying network.

In the rest of this chapter, using the *Shortest-Path* program in Figure 2.5 as the primary example, the extensions to both the data and query model of traditional Datalog in order to handle the requirements of distributed computations (Section 2.3) are presented, namely: soft-state data and rules (Section 2.4), and incremental maintenance of network state (Section 2.5).

2.3   DISTRIBUTED COMPUTATION

From a database perspective, one novelty of declarative networking's setting is that data are distributed and relations may be partitioned across sites. NDlog gives the program writer *explicit* control of data placement with the use of *location specifiers* in each predicate.

Definition 2.1   *A* location specifier *is a field in a predicate whose value per tuple indicates the network storage location of that tuple.*

The location specifier field is of type address, having a value that represents a network location. It is used as a partitioning field for its table across all nodes in the network, similar to horizontally partitioned tables in distributed databases [Özsu and Valduriez, 2011]. We require that each predicate has a single location specifier field that is notated by an "@" symbol. For example, the location specifier of link(@S,D,C) is @S. This means that all link tuples are stored based on the address value of the @S field.

Given that predicates have location specifiers, *local* and *distributed* rules can now be distinguished as follows.

Definition 2.2   Local rules *are rules that have the same location specifier in each predicate, including the head.*

Non-local rules are otherwise known as *distributed rules*. Local rules can be executed without any distributed logic. In the *Shortest-Path* program, rules sp1, sp3 and sp4 are local, while sp2 is a distributed rule since the link and path body predicates are stored at different locations.

2.4   SOFT-STATE DATA AND RULES

Types of relations and rules are distinguished based on *hard-state* and *soft-state* storage models. In the rest of this section, the *Ping-Pong* program in Figure 2.6 is used to illustrate NDlog rules that manipulate soft-state data. Figure 2.7 presents the schemas and meanings of the predicates.

---

materialize(link,10,infinity,keys(1,2)).
materialize(pingRTT,10,5,keys(1,2)).
materialize(pendingPing,10,5,keys(1,2)).
pp1 ping(@S,D,E) :- periodic(@S,E,5), link(@S,D).
pp2 pingMsg(S,@D,E) :- ping(@S,D,E), link(@S,D).
pp3 pendingPing(@S,D,E,T) :- ping(@S,D,E), T = f_now().
pp4 pongMsg(@S,E) :- pingMsg(S,@D,E), link(@D,S).
pp5 pingRTT(@S,D,RTT) :- pongMsg(@S,E), pendingPing(@S,D,E,T),
                         RTT = f_now() - T.
pp6 link(@S,D) :- pingRTT(@S,D,RTT).
Query pingRTT(@S,D,RTT).

Figure 2.6: Ping-Pong NDlog program.

The *Ping-Pong* program implements a simple ping program where each node periodically pings its neighbor nodes to compute the round-trip time (RTT). Unlike the earlier *Shortest-Path* program, all relations used in the *Ping-Pong* program are declared with finite lifetimes and sizes. There are also some relations such as ping, pingMsg and pongMsg that are not declared using the materialize keyword. These relations are known as *event relations*, and they consist of zero-lifetime tuples that are used to execute rules but are not stored.

Predicate	Schema
link(@S,D,E)	link(@Source,Destination,EventID)
ping(@S,D,E)	ping(@Source,Destination,EventID)
pingMsg(S,@D,E)	pingMsg(Source,@Destination,EventID)
pongMsg(@S,E)	pongMsg(@Source,EventID)
pendingPing(@S,D,E,T)	pendingPing(@Source,Destination,EventID,Time)
pingRTT(@S,D,RTT)	pingRTT(@Source,Destination,RoundTripTime)

Figure 2.7: Schema of tables and events used in the *Ping-Pong* program

Rule pp1 is triggered periodically using the special `periodic` predicate. The `periodic(@S,E,5)` predicate denotes an infinite stream of `periodic` event tuples generated at node S every five seconds with random identifier E. This allows rule pp1 to generate at five second intervals, a `ping(@S,D,E)` event tuple at source node S to all its neighbors with destination D. Each `ping` is uniquely identified with an event identifier E. Each `ping` tuple is then used to generate a `pingMsg(S,@D,E)` tuple that is sent to destination node D (rule pp2). A `pendingPing(@S,D,E,T)` tuple is also stored locally to record the creation time T of `ping(@S,D,E)`.

In rule pp4, whenever a node D receives a `pingMsg(S,@D,E)` tuple from the source node S, it replies with a `pongMsg(@S,E)` tuple to node S. Upon receiving the `pingMsg(@S,E)` tuple, rule pp5 is used by node S to compute the RTT between itself and node D based on the time recorded in `pendingPing(@S,D,E,T)`. A successful reply to a ping message indicates that the neighbor is alive. This results in the refresh of link tuples in rule pp6.

2.4.1   HARD-STATE VS. SOFT-STATE DATA

NDlog distinguishes between hard-state and soft-state relations based on the lifetime parameter in `materialized` statements.

Definition 2.3   *A* hard-state relation *is one that is materialized with infinite lifetime.*

Hard-state relations are similar to data stored in traditional databases, which are non-expiring and have to be deleted explicitly. The `link` relation in the *Shortest-Path* program is an example of a hard-state relation. All `link` tuples persist unless explicitly deleted. For derivations such as `path` in the *Shortest-Path-Hop* program, there can be multiple derivations for the same tuple. Hence, one needs to keep track of all such derivations for hard-state relations unless all derivations are invalidated due to deletions.

Definition 2.4   *A* soft-state relation *is one that is materialized with finite lifetime.*

Tuples that are inserted into soft-state tables are stored only for the duration of the table's lifetime. If required by the network protocol, these soft-state tuples can be refreshed via NDlog rules.

Unlike hard-state relations, there is no need to keep track of multiple derivations of the same tuple. Instead, a *refresh* occurs when the same tuple is inserted into the table, resulting in the extension of the tuple by its specified lifetime. For example, the `link` relation in the *Ping-Pong* program is a soft-state relation, and all `link` tuples generated are deleted after ten seconds unless they are refreshed by rule pp6 before they expire.

Definition 2.5   *An* event relation *is a soft-state relation with zero lifetime.*

Event relations can either be declared explicitly via `materialize` statements with the lifetime parameter set to 0, or implicitly if they are not declared in any `materialize` statements. Event relations are typically used to represent message "streams" (e.g., `pingMsg`, `pongMsg` in the *Ping-Pong* program), or periodically generated local events via a built-in `periodic` predicate (e.g., in rule pp1):

Definition 2.6   *The* `periodic(@N,E,T,K)` *event relation is a built-in relation that represents a stream of event tuples generated at node N every T seconds (up to an optional K times) with a random event identifier E. If K is omitted, the stream is generated infinitely.*

Built-in streams in NDLog are akin to the *foreign functions* of LDL++ [Arni et al., 2003] or the table functions of SQL, but their storage semantics are those of events, as described above. For example, the `periodic(@S,E,5)` in rule pp1 denotes an infinite stream of `periodic` event tuples generated at node S every 5 seconds with random identifier E.

2.4.2   HARD-STATE AND SOFT-STATE RULES

Following the definitions of hard-state and soft-state data, this section presents *hard-state rules* and *soft-state rules*, which differ on their use of hard-state and soft-state relations in the rules:

Definition 2.7   *A* hard-state rule *contains only hard-state predicates in the rule head and body.*

Definition 2.8   *A* soft-state rule *contains at least one soft-state predicate in the rule head or body.*

Soft-state rules are further classified as follows.

Definition 2.9   *A* pure soft-state rule *has a soft-state predicate in the rule head, and at least one soft-state predicate in the rule body.*

Definition 2.10   *A* derived soft-state rule *has a soft-state predicate in the rule head, but only hard-state predicates in the rule body.*

Definition 2.11 *An* archival soft-state rule *has a hard-state rule head, and at least one soft-state predicate in the rule body.*

Archival soft-state rules are primarily used for archival or logging purposes. These rules derive hard-state tuples that persist even after the input soft-state tuples that generate them have expired.

Since event relations are considered soft-state relations (with zero lifetimes), they can be used in any of the three soft-state rules above. During rule execution, input event tuples persist long enough for rule execution to complete and are then discarded. Since they are not stored, NDlog does not model the possibility of two instantaneous events occurring simultaneously. Syntactically, this possibility is prevented by allowing no more than one event predicate in soft-state rule bodies:

Definition 2.12 *An* event soft-state rule *is a soft-state rule with* exactly one *event predicate in the rule body.*

Using the *Ping-Pong* program as example, all rules are pure soft-state relations since no hard-state relations are used in this program. In addition, rules `pp1-pp5` are event soft-state rules that take as input one event predicate (`periodic`, `ping`, `ping`, `pingMsg` and `pongMsg` respectively).

2.5   INCREMENTAL MAINTENANCE OF NETWORK STATE

As in network protocols, NDlog rules are designed to be executed over a period of time and incrementally updated based on changes in the underlying network. During rule execution, depending on their specified lifetimes, all derived tuples are either stored in materialized table or generated as events. All materialized derivations have to be incrementally recomputed by long-running NDlog rules in order to maintain consistency with changes in the input base tables.

For hard-state rules, this involves the straightforward application of traditional materialized view maintenance techniques [Gupta et al., 1993]. Consider three types of modifications to hard-state relations: insertions of new tuples, deletions of existing tuples, and updates (which can be modeled as deletion followed by an insertion). Note that inserting a tuple where there is another tuple with the same primary key is considered an update, where the existing tuple is deleted before the new one is inserted.

As with traditional database materialized views, the deletions of any input relations result in *cascaded deletions*, which leads to the deletion of previously derived tuples. For example, whenever a `link` tuple is deleted, all `path` tuples that are generated using this `link` tuple have to be deleted as well. Since there can be multiple derivations of each unique tuple, one needs to keep track of all of them and only delete a tuple when all its derivations are deleted.

The incremental maintenance of soft-state rules is carried out in a slightly different fashion due to the presence of soft-state relations. Two types of modifications are considered: insertions of new tuples or *refreshes* of existing soft-state tuples. Recall from Section 2.4.1 that a *refresh* occurs when the same tuple is inserted into the table, resulting in the extension of the tuple by its specified lifetime. These soft-state refreshes in turn lead to *cascaded refreshes*, where previously derived soft-state tuples are rederived and hence also refreshed. Unlike the maintenance of hard-state rules, cascaded deletions do not occur in soft-state rules. Instead, all derived soft-state tuples are stored for their specified lifetimes and timeout in a manner consistent with traditional soft-state semantics.

2.6   SUMMARY OF NETWORK DATALOG

Given the above preliminaries, the NDlog data model is based on the relational model with the following constraints.

1. All NDlog relations are horizontally partitioned in the network based on the location specifier attribute.

2. An NDlog relation is either a hard-state or soft-state relation depending on its lifetime.

An NDlog program is a Datalog program that satisfies the following syntactic constraints.

1. All predicates in an NDlog rule head or rule body have a location specifier attribute.

2. An NDlog rule is either a hard-state or soft-state rule.

In addition, the results of executing NDlog rules are materialized for their table lifetimes, and incrementally maintained as described in Section 2.5.

Interestingly, NDlog uses a somewhat more physical data model than the relational model, and a correspondingly somewhat more physical language. The main reason for doing this is to capture the essence of a network protocol—communication over links—in a way that remains largely declarative, leaving significant latitude for a compiler to choose an implementation of the specification. Note that most aspects of a program other than storage location and communication pairs are left unspecified—this includes the order in which tuples of a set are handled and the order in which predicates of a rule are considered. In addition, the need for partitioning via location specifiers reflects low-level networks. In principle, given a network implemented in this manner to achieve all-pairs communication, higher-level logic could be written without reference to locations or links. This is a natural extension to NDlog, and has since been explored in subsequent language extensions [Mao et al., 2008, Marczak et al., 2010].

2.7   SUMMARY

This chapter formally defined the NDlog language. The NDlog language is based on Datalog, and includes extensions to address NDlog's three main requirements of *distributed computation, support for soft-state data and rules,* and *incremental maintenance of network state*. All of these extensions have been motivated by the distributed settings targeted in declarative networking, which are a departure from the environments in which traditional Datalog was used. The subsequent chapters then present two concrete instances of declarative networking, namely *declarative routing* and *declarative overlays,* and describe in detail how NDlog programs are processed and executed to implement the network protocols.

CHAPTER 3

Declarative Networking Overview

Having presented a variety of declarative routing protocols using NDlog, the next two chapters describe how NDlog programs can be compiled and executed to implement the network protocols. This chapter in particular is primarily focused on providing an overview of a declarative networking (DN) engine implementation, largely drawn from the experiences of the P2 system [P2]. The next chapter will focus specifically on the system component that processes NDlog programs.

The chapter is organized as follows. Section 3.1 presents the architectural overview of a DN engine and its different components. Section 3.2 describes the runtime engine used by declarative networking. Section 3.3 shows how network state is stored and managed as tables. The chapter concludes in Section 3.3.1 with a description of RapidNet, a recent successor of the P2 system.

3.1 ARCHITECTURE

Figure 3.1 shows the architecture of a declarative networking system from the perspective of a single node. There are three main components: the *planner*, *dataflow installer*, and *dataflow engine*. The DN engine utilizes a dataflow framework at runtime for maintaining network state. DN dataflows are similar to database query plans, which consist of graphs that connect various database "operators" with dataflow edges that represent the passing of tuples among operators, possibly across a network.

To implement a network protocol, the planner takes as input the network specification expressed as a NDlog program, and compiles the program into a dataflow graph. In order to disseminate NDlog programs throughout a network, a DN runtime system provides simple mechanisms for each node to send input NDlog programs by flooding its neighbors. When a dataflow is installed (i.e., the planner has created and inter-connected the database operators according to the compiled dataflow), all the required *local tables* and indices necessary for the program are also created. Indices are created for every table's primary key, and additional indices are constructed on any table columns that are involved in unification (relational join). Once installed, dataflows are executed by the runtime engine until they are explicitly canceled.

The execution of the dataflow graph results in the implementation of the network protocol itself. The dataflow graph is registered locally at each node's dataflow engine via a *dataflow installer*. Each local dataflow participates in a global, *distributed* dataflow, with messages flowing among dataflows executed at different nodes, resulting in updates to the network state used by the network protocol. The distributed dataflow when executed performs the operations of a network protocol.

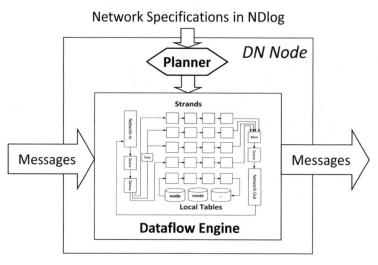

Figure 3.1: Components of a single declarative networking node.

The local tables store the state of the network protocols, and the flow of messages entering and leaving the dataflow constitute the network messages generated by the executing protocol.

3.2   DN DATAFLOW ENGINE

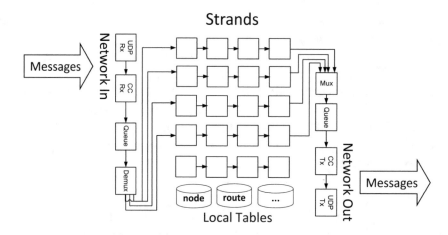

Figure 3.2: Dataflow example at a single node.

The dataflow engine of DN was inspired by prior work in both databases and networking. Software dataflow architectures occupy a constrained but surprisingly rich design space that has been explored in a variety of contexts. Dataflow graphs have been used previously by parallel and distributed database query systems like Gamma [DeWitt et al., 1986], Volcano [Graefe, 1990] and PIER [Huebsch et al., 2005] as their basic query executables.

The use of the dataflow framework has recently been explored in related work on extensible networks. For example, software router toolkits like Scout [Mosberger and Peterson, 1996], Click [Kohler et al., 2000] and XORP [Handley et al., 2005] in recent years have demonstrated that network message handling and protocol implementation can be neatly factored into dataflow diagrams. This book adopts the Click term *element* for a node in a DN dataflow graph, but as in database query plans, each edge in the graph carries a stream of well structured tuples, rather than annotated IP packets. Note that while all tuples flowing on a single edge share a structure (schema), tuples on one edge may have very different structure than tuples on another – this is a significant distinction with the uniform IP packets of Click.

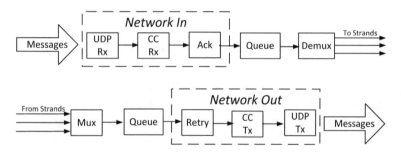

Figure 3.3: Example of expanded *Network-In* and *Network-Out* elements.

Figure 3.2 shows an example of a DN dataflow being executed at a single node. At the edges of the dataflow, a chain of network packet processing elements (encapsulated in the figure as *Network-In* and *Network-Out*) are used to process incoming and outgoing messages respectively. Figure 3.3 shows an example implementation of the networking-related elements. Both the *Network-In* and *Network-Out* portion of the dataflow comprise a longer sequence of network-related elements that implement functionality for sending and receiving messages using the UDP transmission protocol (*UDP-Tx* and *UDP-Rx*), and may also perform reliable transmission (*Retry* and *Ack*), and congestion control (*CC-Tx* and *CC-Rx* elements). These elements can be dynamically adapted (reordered, added or removed from the dataflow) based on the requirements of the declarative network [Condie et al., 2005].

Messages that arrive into the dataflow are buffered using queues, and demultiplexed (using the *Demux* element) via the relation name of each tuple into *strands*, and then duplicated (using the *Dup* element) into multiple strands that require input from the same relation. The strands are directly compiled from NDlog rules and implement the "logic" of the network. Each strand consists of a chain of elements implementing relational database operators like joins, selections, projections and aggregations. The use of joins is endemic in declarative networking because of the choice of NDlog: the unification (matching) of variables in the body of a rule is implemented in a dataflow by an equality-based relational join (*equijoin*). As shown in Figure 3.2, these strands take as input tuples that arrive via the network (output from the *Dup* element), local table updates (directly from the local tables) or local periodically generated events. The execution of strands either results in local table updates, or the sending of message tuples.

On the other side of the graph (shown as the *Network-Out* elements), message tuples are merged by a *Mux* element, queued and then sent based on their network destinations. Remote tuples are sent via an output queue to the network stack to be packetized, marshaled, and buffered by DN's UDP transport, while tuples destined for local consumption are "wrapped around" to the *Network-In* element and queued along with other input tuples arriving over the network.

At runtime, the *Network-In* and *Network-Out* elements can be shared by multiple overlays that run concurrently. The system will compile them into a single dataflow for execution, where the *Network-In* and *Network-Out* elements will be shared among the different overlays.

3.2.1　DATAFLOW ELEMENTS

This section gives a brief overview of the suite of dataflow elements implemented in DN. As in Click, nodes in a DN dataflow graph can be chosen from a set of C++ objects called *elements*. In database systems these are often called *operators*, since they derive from logical operators in the relational algebra. DN provides the relational operators found in most database systems, as well as query processors like PIER [Huebsch et al., 2005]: selection, projection, streaming relational join operations such as pipelined hash-joins [Wilschut and Apers, 1991], "group-by," and various aggregation functions.

One example of this is in DN's networking stack. Systems like PIER [Huebsch et al., 2005] abstract details of transport protocols, message formats, marshaling, etc., away from the dataflow framework, and operators only deal with fully unmarshaled tuples. In contrast, DN explicitly uses the dataflow model to chain together separate elements responsible for socket handling, packet scheduling, congestion control, reliable transmission, data serialization, and dispatch [Condie et al., 2005].

A variety of elements form a bridge between the dataflow graph and persistent state in the form of stored tables. DN has elements that store incoming tuples in tables, lookup elements that can iteratively emit all tuples in a table matching a search filter, and aggregation elements that maintain an up-to-date aggregate (such as max, min, count, etc.) on a table and emit it whenever it changes. Tables are frequently shared between elements, although some elements generate their own private tables. For example, the element responsible for eliminating duplicate results in a dataflow uses a table to keep track of what it has seen so far. Finally, for debugging purposes, print elements that can be inserted to "watch" tuples based on table name (specified via a special "`watch(tableName)`" statement within the NDlog program) entering and leaving the dataflow.

3.3   NETWORK STATE STORAGE AND MANAGEMENT

Network state is stored in *tables*, which contain tuples with expiry times and size constraints that are declaratively specified at table creation time as described in Chapter 2. Duplicate entries (tuples) are allowed in tables, and the mechanisms for maintaining these duplicates differ based on whether they are hard-state or soft-state tables as defined in Chapter 2. In *hard-state* tables, a derivation count is maintained for each unique tuple, and each tuple is deleted when its count reaches zero. In *soft-state* tables, each unique tuple has an associated lifetime that is set based on the specified expiration of its table during creation time. Duplicates result in extension of tuple lifetime, and each tuple is deleted upon expiration based on its lifetime. The lifetimes of soft-state tuples are enforced by purging the soft-state tables of any expired tuples whenever they are accessed. Tables are named using unique IDs, and consequently can be shared between different queries and/or dataflow elements.

As basic data types, DN uses `Values`, and `Tuples`. A `Value` is a reference-counted object used to pass around any scalar item in the system; `Value` types include strings, integers, timestamps, and large unique identifiers. The `Value` class, together with the rules for converting between the various value types, constitute the concrete type system of DN. A `Tuple` is a vector of `Values`, and is the basic unit of data transfer in DN. Dataflow elements, described below, pass tuples between them, and tables hold sets of tuples.

Queries over tables can be specified by filters, providing an expressivity roughly equivalent to a traditional database query over a single table. In-memory indices (implemented using standard hash tables) can be attached to attributes of tables to enable quick equality lookups. Note that the table implementation—including associated indices—is a node-local construct.

3.3.1   RAPIDNET DECLARATIVE NETWORKING ENGINE

The *RapidNet* [RapidNet] declarative networking engine compile the NDlog programs into applications (with an execution model similar to Click [Kohler et al., 2000]) executable in *ns-3* [ns-3], an emerging discrete event-driven simulator similar to the popular *ns-2*. Like its predecessor, *ns-3* emulates all layers of the network stack, supporting configurable loss, packet queuing, and network topology models.

RapidNet has been used as an experimental platform [Liu et al., 2012, Muthukumar et al., 2009a] for a variety of declarative wireless routing protocols on the ORBIT [ORBIT] wireless testbed. The ability to run the same application in these two modes enables us to execute each NDlog program at scale in simulation and in an actual implementation running on a testbed.

In the initial design phase of *RapidNet*, a network protocol design is used as the basis for specifying the network protocol using the NDlog declarative networking language. In the *simulation mode*, the *RapidNet* compilation process generates ns-3 code from the NDlog protocol specifications. The generated code either runs as an ns-3 application, or replaces routing protocol implementations at the network layer. In the *implementation mode*, declarative networking specifications are directly executed and deployed either by using actual network sockets implemented on a real network across multiple machines. Simulation mode enables a comprehensive examination under various network topologies and conditions, while the implementation mode allows different hosts in a testbed environment to execute the deployed system over a real network.

Since declarative networks share common functionalities such as the network stack, multiplexing tuple messages entering and leaving the dataflow, and database functionalities, all these utilities are defined in a shared *RapidNet* library. This enables one to simplify the compilation process to only the relevant database operations to implement the distributed dataflows for the corresponding declarative network specification. This also enables one to easily incorporate *multi-query optimizations* to share computations across declarative networks in future.

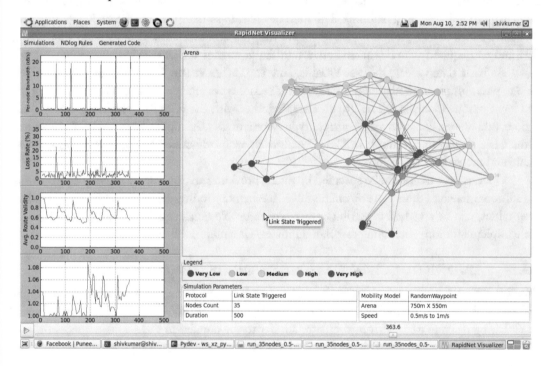

Figure 3.4: RapidNet demonstration [Muthukumar et al., 2009a,b] of a link-state routing protocol.

The *RapidNet* system takes input declarative network specifications which are automatically compiled to ns-3 code for execution in the ns-3 simulation and emulation modes. Network traces are directed to a ns-3 visualizer that will display the actual movement of nodes during the simulation, and side-by-side actual performance statistics of the protocol obtained from the ns-3 network statistics package.

Figure 3.4 shows an example execution of *RapidNet* system, based on a declarative mobile ad-hoc network (MANET) routing protocol [Liu et al., 2009a, 2011a]. The system (as demonstrated in [Muthukumar et al., 2009b]) visually shows the actual movements of nodes communicating via 802.11b ad-hoc mode using one of ns-3's supported mobility models (e.g., random waypoint,

Brownian motion, hierarchical mobility, etc.). Each *RapidNet* node incrementally updates its routes using a variety of declarative MANET routing protocols such as hazy-sighted link-state routing (HSLS) [Santivanez et al., 2001], optimized link-state routing (OLSR) [Clausen and Jacquet, 2003], dynamic source routing (DSR) [Johnson and Maltz, 1996], and summary-vector based epidemic routing [Vahdat and Becker, 2000]. Actual performance statistics of the protocol are also displayed side-by-side the actual protocol itself.

3.4   SUMMARY

This chapter presents an overview of the DN declarative networking engine, with an emphasis on its architecture, various components (planner, dataflow installer, dataflow engine), dataflow framework and network state management. The next chapter describes the *planner* component in greater detail, and shows how NDlog programs can be compiled into dataflow-based execution plans to implement the network protocols using the DN dataflow engine.

CHAPTER 4

Distributed Recursive Query Processing

One of the main challenges of using a declarative language is to ensure that the declarative specifications, when compiled and executed, result in correct and efficient implementations that are faithful to the program specifications. This is particularly challenging in a distributed context, where asynchronous messaging and the unannounced failure of participants make it hard to reason about the flow of data and events in the system as a whole. This chapter addresses this challenge by describing the steps required for the DN planner to automatically and correctly generate execution plans from the NDlog rules.

4.1 CENTRALIZED PLAN GENERATION

This section describes the steps required to generate execution plans of a centralized Datalog program using the *semi-naïve* (SN) fixpoint evaluation mechanism [Balbin and Ramamohanarao, 1987]. SN is the standard method used to evaluate Datalog programs correctly with no redundant computations. The *Shortest-Path* program (Figure 2.5 in Chapter 2) is used here as an example of how SN is achieved in the DN engine.

4.1.1 SEMI-NAÏVE EVALUATION

The first step in SN is the *semi-naïve rewrite*, where each Datalog rule is rewritten to generate a number of *delta rules* to be evaluated. Consider the following rule:

$$p :- p_1, p_2, ..., p_n, b_1, b_2, ..., b_m. \tag{4.1}$$

$p_1, ..., p_n$ are *derived predicates* and $b_1, ..., b_m$ are *base predicates*. Derived predicates refer to intensional relations that are derived during rule execution. Base predicates refer to extensional (stored) relations whose values are not changed during rule execution. The SN rewrite generates n *delta rules*, one for each derived predicate, where the kth delta rule has the form[1]:

$$\triangle p^{new} :- p_1^{old}, ..., p_{k-1}^{old}, \triangle p_k^{old}, p_{k+1}, ..., p_n, b_1, b_2, ..., b_m. \tag{4.2}$$

---

[1]These delta rules are logically equivalent to rules of the form $\triangle p_j^{new} :- p_1, p_2, ..., p_{k-1}, \triangle p_k^{old}, p_{k+1}, ..., p_n, b_1, b_2, ..., b_m$, and have the advantage of avoiding redundant inferences within each iteration.

In each delta rule, $\triangle p_k^{old}$ is the *delta predicate*, and refers to p_k tuples generated for the first time in the previous iteration. Here, p_k^{old} refers to all p_k tuples generated before the previous iteration. For example, the following rule r2-1 is the delta rule for the recursive rule r2 from the Datalog program shown in Figure 2.1 from Chapter 2:

$$\triangle path^{new}(S, D, Z, C) : - link(S, Z, C1), \triangle path^{old}(Z, D, Z2, C2), C = C1 + C2. \quad (4.3)$$

The only derived predicate in rule r2 is path, and hence one delta rule is generated. All the delta rules generated from the rewrite are then executed in synchronous rounds (or iterations) of computation, where input tuples computed in the previous iteration of a recursive rule execution are used as input in the current iteration to compute new tuples. Any new tuples that are generated for the first time in the current iteration are then used as input to the next iteration. This is repeated until a fixpoint is achieved (i.e., no new tuples are produced).

Algorithm 4.1 summarizes the basic semi-naïve evaluation used to execute these rules in the DN engine. In this algorithm, DN maintains a buffer for each delta rule, denoted by B_k. This buffer is used to store p_k tuples generated in the previous iteration ($\triangle p_k^{old}$). Initially, p_k, p_k^{old}, $\triangle p_k^{old}$ and $\triangle p_k^{new}$ are empty. As a base case, all rules are executed to generate the initial p_k tuples, which are inserted into the corresponding B_k buffers. Each iteration of the while loop consists of flushing all existing $\triangle p_k^{old}$ tuples from B_k and executing all the delta rules to generate $\triangle p_j^{new}$ tuples, which are used to update p_j^{old}, B_j and p_j accordingly. Note that only new p_j tuples generated in the current iteration are inserted into B_j for use in the next iteration. A fixpoint is reached when all buffers are empty.

Algorithm 4.1 Semi-naïve Evaluation in DN

---

execute all rules
for each derived predicate p_k
    $B_k \leftarrow p_k$
end
while $\exists B_k.size > 0$
        $\forall B_k$ where $B_k.size > 0$, $\triangle p_k^{old} \leftarrow B_k.flush()$
        execute all delta rules
        for each derived predicate p_j
            $p_j^{old} \leftarrow p_j^{old} \cup \triangle p_j^{old}$
            $B_j \leftarrow \triangle p_j^{new} - p_j^{old}$
            $p_j \leftarrow p_j^{old} \cup B_j$
            $\triangle p_j^{new} \leftarrow \emptyset$
        end
end

4.1.2   DATAFLOW GENERATION

Algorithm 4.1 requires executing the delta rules at every iteration. These delta rules are each compiled into an execution plan, which is in the form of a DN dataflow *strand*, using the conventions of the DN dataflow framework described in Chapter 3. Each dataflow strand implements a delta rule via a chain of relational operators. In the rest of this chapter, the dataflow strand for each delta rule is referred to as a *rule strand*.

For each delta rule, each rule strand takes as input its *delta predicate* (prepended with $\triangle$). This input is then used as input to the strand which implements a sequence of elements implementing relational equijoins. Since tables are implemented as main-memory data structures with local indices over them, tuples from the stream are pushed into an equijoin element, and all matches in the table are found via an index lookup.

After the translation of the equijoins in a rule, the planner creates elements for any selection filters, which evaluate the selection predicate over each tuple, dropping those for which the result is false. In some cases, the dataflow can be optimized to push a selection upstream of an equijoin, to limit the state and work in the equijoin, following traditional database rules on the commutativity of join and selection.

Aggregate operations like MIN or COUNT are translated after equijoins and selections, since they operate on fields in the rule head. Aggregate elements generally hold internal state, and when a new tuple arrives, compute the aggregate incrementally. The final part of translating each rule is the addition of a "projection" element that constructs a tuple matching the head of the rule.

$\triangle path^{new}(S,D,Z,C) :- link(S,Z,C1), \triangle path^{old}(Z,D,Z2,C2), C = C1 + C2.$

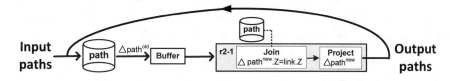

Figure 4.1: Rule strand for delta rule r2-1 in DN.

Figure 4.1 shows the dataflow realization for delta rule r2-1. The rule is repeated above the dataflow for convenience. The example rule strand receives new $\triangle path^{old}$ tuples generated in the previous iteration to generate new paths ($\triangle path^{new}$) which are then "wrapped-around" and inserted into the path table (with duplicate elimination) for further processing in the next iteration. In effect, semi-naïve evaluation achieves the computation of paths in synchronous rounds of increasing hop counts, where paths that have been previously derived in the previous round are used to generate new paths in the next iteration.

4.2   DISTRIBUTED PLAN GENERATION

In this section, we demonstrate the steps required to generate the execution plans for distributed NDlog rules. In Chapter 2, we introduced the concept of distributed NDlog rules, where the rule body predicates have different location specifiers. These distributed rules cannot be executed at a single node, since the tuples that must be joined are situated at different nodes in the network. Prior to the SN rewrite step, an additional *localization rewrite* step ensures that all body predicates for tuples to be joined are at the same node. After applying the localization rewrite to all distributed rules, all localized rules will have rule bodies that are locally computable and hence can be processed in a similar fashion as centralized Datalog rules.

> sp2 path(@S,D,Z,P,C) :- link(@S,Z,C1), path(@Z,D,Z2,P2,C2), C = C1 + C2,
> P = f_concatPath(S,P2).

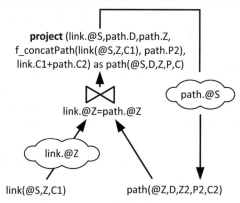

Figure 4.2: Logical query plan for distributed rule sp2 shown above the figure.

4.2.1   LOCALIZATION REWRITE

To provide a high-level intuition for the localization rewrite, we consider the distributed rule sp2 from the *Shortest-Path* program presented in Chapter 2. This rule is distributed because the link and path predicates in the rule body have different location specifiers, but are joined by a common "Z" field. Figure 4.2 shows the corresponding logical query plan depicting the distributed join. The clouds represent an "exchange"-like operator [Graefe, 1990] that forwards tuples from one network node to another; clouds are labeled with the link attribute that determines the tuple's recipient. The first cloud (link.@Z) sends link tuples to the neighbor nodes indicated by their destination address fields. The second cloud (path.@S) transmits new path tuples computed from the join for further processing, setting the recipient according to the source address field.

Based on the above distributed join, rule sp2 can be rewritten into the following two rules. Note that all predicates in the body of sp2a have the same location specifiers; the same is true of sp2b. Since `linkD` is derived from the materialized table `link`, we need to also declare `linkD` via the `materialize` statement, and set its lifetime and size parameters to be the same as that of the `link` table.

---

materialize(linkD,infinity,infinity,1,2).
sp2a linkD(S,@Z,C) :- link(@S,Z,C).
sp2b path(@S,D,Z,P,C) :- link(@Z,S,C3),linkD(S,@Z,C1),path(@Z,D,Z2,P2,C2),
                    C = C1 + C2, P = f_concatPath(S,P2).

Figure 4.3: Localized rules for distributed rule `sp2`.

The rewrite is achievable because the `link` and `path` predicates, although at different locations, share a common join address field.

4.2.2   DISTRIBUTED DATAFLOW GENERATION

---

sp2a $\triangle linkD^{new}(S,@Z,C)$:- $\triangle link^{old}(@S,Z,C)$.
sp2b-1 $\triangle path^{new}(@S,D,Z,P,C)$:- link(@Z,S,C3), linkD(S,@Z,C1),
                    $\triangle path^{old}(@Z,D,Z2,P2,C2)$, C = C1 + C2,
                    $P = f\_concat Path(S,P2)$.
sp2b-2 $\triangle path^{new}(@S,D,Z,P,C)$:- link(@Z,S,C3), $\triangle linkD^{old}(S,@Z,C1)$,
                    path(@Z,D,Z2,P2,C2), C = C1 + C2,
                    $P = f\_concat Path(S,P2)$.

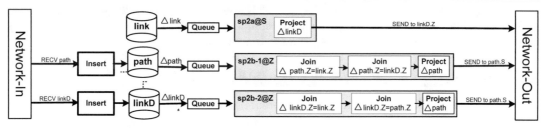

Figure 4.4: Delta rules and compiled rule strands for localized rules `sp2a` and `sp2b`.

After rule localization, the SN rewrite described in Section 4.1.1 is used to generate delta rules that are compiled into rule strands. In Figure 4.4, we provide an example of the delta rules and compiled rule strands for the localized rules `sp2a` and `sp2b` shown in Figure 4.3.

In addition to creating the relational operations described in the previous section on rule strand generation, the planner also constructs the other portions of the dataflow graph in order to support distribution. These are the network processing elements, which include multiplexing and demultiplexing tuples, marshaling, unmarshaling and congestion control. As with Click [Kohler et al.,

2000], it also inserts explicit queue elements where there is a push/pull mismatch between two elements that need to be connected.

For simplicity, we represent the network packet processing, demultiplexing and multiplexing elements described in Section 3.2 as *Network-In* and *Network-Out* blocks in the figure, and only show the elements for the rule strands. Unlike the centralized strand in Figure 4.1, there are now three rule strands. The extra two strands (sp2a@S and sp2b-2@Z) are used as follows. Rule strand sp2a@S sends all existing links to the destination address field as `linkD` tuples. Rule strand sp2b-2@Z takes the new `linkD` tuples it received via the network, stores them using the *Insert element*. Each new `linkD` tuple (with duplicate elimination) is then used to perform a join operation with the local `path` table to generate new paths.

4.3 RELAXING SEMI-NAÏVE EVALUATION

In the distributed implementation, the execution of rule strands can depend on tuples arriving via the network, and can also result in new tuples being sent over the network. Traditional SN completely evaluates all rules on a given set of facts, i.e., completes the *iteration*, before considering any new facts. In a distributed execution environment where messages can be delayed or lost, the completion of an iteration in the traditional sense can only be detected by a consensus computation across multiple nodes, which is prohibitively expensive. Further, the requirement that many nodes complete the iteration together (a "barrier synchronization" in parallel computing terminology) limits parallelism significantly by restricting the rate of progress to that of the slowest node.

We address this by making the notion of iteration local to a node. New facts might be generated through local rule execution, or might be received from another node while a local iteration is in progress. The *pipelined semi-naive* (PSN) extends SN to work in an asynchronous distributed setting, while generating the same results as SN. These techniques avoid duplicate inferences [Loo, 2006], which would otherwise result in generating unnecessary network messages.

4.3.1 PIPELINED SEMI-NAÏVE EVALUATION

Pipelined SN (PSN) relaxes SN to the extreme of processing each tuple as it is received. This provides opportunities for additional optimizations on a per-tuple basis, at the potential cost of batch, set-oriented optimizations of local processing. New tuples that are generated from the SN rules, as well as tuples received from other nodes, are used immediately to compute tuples without waiting for the current (local) iteration to complete.

Algorithm 4.2 shows the pseudocode for PSN. The kth delta rule is of the form:

$$p_j^{new,i+1} :- p_1, ..., p_{k-1}, t_k^{old,i}, p_{k+1}, ..., p_n, b_1, b_2, ..., b_m. \tag{4.4}$$

Each tuple, denoted t, has a superscript (old/new, i) where i is its corresponding iteration number in SN. Each processing step in PSN consists of dequeuing a tuple $t_k^{old,i}$ from Q_k and then using it as input into all corresponding rule strands. Each resulting $t_j^{new,i+1}$ tuple is pipelined, stored in

Algorithm 4.2 Pipelined SN (PSN) Evaluation.

---

execute all rules

for each $t_k \in$ derived predicate p_k

    $t_k.T \leftarrow$ current_time()

    $B_k \leftarrow t_k$

end

while $\exists Q_k.size > 0$

    $t_k^{old,i} \leftarrow Q_k.dequeueTuple()$

    for each delta rule execution

        $\triangle p_j^{new,i+1} :- p_1, p_2, ..., p_{k-1}, t_k^{old,i}, p_{k+1}, .., p_n, b_1, b_2, ..., b_m,$

        $t^{old,i}.T \geq p_1.T, t^{old,i}.T \geq p_2.T, ..., t^{old,i}.T \geq p_{k-1}.T, t^{old,i}.T \geq p_{k+1}.T, ...,$

        $t^{old,i}.T \geq p_n.T, t^{old,i}.T \geq b_1.T., t^{old,i}.T \geq b_2.T, ..., t^{old,i}.T \geq b_m.T$

        for each $t_j^{new,i+1} \in \triangle p_j^{new,i+1}$

            if $t_j^{new,i+1} \notin p_j$

                then $p_j \leftarrow p_j \cup t_j^{new,i+1}$

                    $t_j^{new,i+1}.T \leftarrow$ current_time()

                    $Q_j.enqueueTuple(t_j^{new,i+1})$

            end

        end

        end

    end

end

---

its respective p_j table (if a copy is not already there), and enqueued into Q_j for further processing. Note that in a distributed implementation, Q_j can be a queue on another node, and the node that receives the new tuple can immediately process the tuple after the enqueue into Q_j. For example, the dataflow in Figure 4.4 is based on a distributed implementation of PSN, where incoming `path` and $linkD$ tuples received via the network are stored locally, and enqueued for processing in the corresponding rule strands.

    To fully pipeline evaluation, we have also removed the distinctions between p_j^{old} and p_j in the rules. Instead, a timestamp (or monotonically increasing sequence number) is added to each tuple upon its arrival (or when inserted into its table), and the join operator matches each tuple only with tuples that have the same or older timestamp. In Algorithm 4.2, we denote the timestamp of each tuple as a T field (assigned via a system call `current_time()`) and add additional selection predicates (highlighted in bold) to the kth delta rule:

$$p_j^{new,i+1} :- p_1, .., p_{k-1}, t_k^{old,i}, p_{k+1}, .., p_n, b_1, b_2, ..., b_m,$$

$$\mathbf{t^{old,i}.T \geq p_1.T, t^{old,i}.T \geq p_2.T, ..., t^{old,i}.T \geq p_{k-1}.T, t^{old,i}.T \geq p_{k+1}.T}, ...,$$

$$t^{old,i}.T \geq p_n.T, t^{old,i}.T \geq b_1.T., t^{old,i}.T \geq b_2.T, ..., t^{old,i}.T \geq b_m.T.$$

Each selection predicate $t^{old,i}.T \geq p_k.T$ ensures that the timestamp of $t^{old,i}$ is greater than or equal to the timestamp of a tuple $t \in p_k$. By relaxing SN, we allow for the processing of tuples immediately upon arrival, which is natural for network message handling. The timestamp represents an alternative "book-keeping" strategy to the rewriting used in SN to ensure no repeated inferences. Note that the timestamp only needs to be assigned locally, since all the rules are localized.

Given a rule with n derived predicates and m base predicates:

$$p : - \ p_1, p_2, ..., p_n, b_1, b_2, ..., b_m. \tag{4.5}$$

It is shown that PSN generates the same results as SN, and does not repeat any inferences [Loo, 2006].

In order to compute rules with aggregation (such as sp3), we utilize incremental fixpoint evaluation techniques [Ramakrishnan et al., 1992] that are amenable to pipelined query processing. These techniques can compute *monotonic aggregates* such as MIN, MAX and COUNT incrementally based on the current aggregate and each new input tuple.

4.4 PROCESSING IN A DYNAMIC NETWORK

In practice, the state of the network is constantly changing during the execution of NDlog programs. In contrast to transactional databases, changes to the network state are not isolated from NDlog programs while they are running. Instead, as in network protocols, NDlog rules are expected to perform dynamic recomputations to reflect the most current state of the network. To better understand the semantics in a dynamic network, we consider the following two degrees of dynamism.

- **Continuous Update Model:** In this model, we assume that updates occur very frequently—at a period that is shorter than the expected time for a typical program to reach a fixpoint. Hence, the query results never fully reflect the state of the network.

- **Bursty Update Model:** In this more constrained (but still fairly realistic) model, updates are allowed to happen during query processing. However, we make the assumption that after a burst of updates, the network eventually *quiesces* (does not change) for a time long enough to allow all the rule computations in the system to reach a fixpoint.

In this discussion, we focus on the bursty model, since it is amenable to analysis; the results on the bursty model provide some intuition as to the behavior in the continuous update model. The goal in the bursty model is to achieve a variant of the typical distributed systems notion of *eventual consistency*, customized to the particulars of NDlog: we wish to ensure that the eventual state of the quiescent system corresponds to what would be achieved by rerunning the rules from scratch in that state. We briefly sketch the ideas here, and follow up with details in the remainder of the section.

To ensure well-defined semantics, we use techniques from materialized view maintenance [Gupta et al., 1993], and consider three types of changes.

- **Insertion:** The insertion of a new tuple at any stage of processing can be naturally handled by (pipelined) semi-naïve evaluation.

- **Deletion:** The deletion of a base tuple leads to the deletion of any tuples that were derived from that base tuple (*cascaded deletions*). Deletions are carried out incrementally via (pipelined) semi-naïve evaluation by incrementally deriving all tuples that are to be deleted.

- **Update:** An update is treated as a deletion followed by an insertion. An update to a base tuple may itself result in derivation of more updates that are propagated via (pipelined) semi-naïve evaluation.

We further allow implicit updates by primary key, where a newly generated tuple replaces an existing tuple with the same primary key (but differs on other fields). The use of pipelined SN evaluation in the discussion can be replaced with buffered SN without changing our analysis. Since some tuples in hard-state tables may have multiple derivations, we make use of the *count algorithm* [Gupta et al., 1993] for keeping track of the number of derivations for each tuple, and only delete a tuple when the count is 0.

4.4.1 DATAFLOW GENERATION FOR INCREMENTAL VIEW MAINTENANCE

Algorithm 4.3 Rule strands generation for incremental insertion of hard-state SN delta rules.

---

for each kth delta rule $\triangle p : - p_1, p_2, ..., \triangle p_k, ..., p_n, b_1, b_2, ..., b_m$
    $RS_{ins} \leftarrow addElement(NULL, Insert\text{-}Listener(\triangle p_k))$
    for each derived predicate p_j where $j \neq k$
        $RS_{ins} \leftarrow addElement(RS_{ins}, Join(p_j))$
    end
    for each base predicate b_j
        $RS_{ins} \leftarrow addElement(RS_{ins}, Join(b_j))$
    end
    $RS_{ins} \leftarrow addElement(RS_{ins}, Project(\triangle p))$
    $RS_{ins} \leftarrow addElement(RS_{ins}, Network\text{-}Out)$
    $RS1_{ins} \leftarrow addElement(NULL, Network\text{-}In(\triangle p))$
    $RS1_{ins} \leftarrow addElement(RS1_{ins}, Insert(\triangle p))$
end

Algorithms 4.3 and 4.4 shows the pseudocode for generating the rule strands for a typical delta rule of the form $\triangle p : - p_1, p_2, ..., \triangle p_k, ..., p_n, b_1, b_2, ..., b_m$, with n derived predicates and m base predicates. The first algorithm generates rule strands RS_{ins} and $RS1_{ins}$ for incremental insertions, and the second algorithm generates rule strands RS_{del} and $RS1_{del}$ for incremental deletions. In both algorithms, the function $RS \leftarrow addElement(RS, element)$ adds an element to the input rule strand RS, and then returns RS itself. For correctness, each strand has to execute completely before another strand is executed.

In Algorithm 4.3, each RS_{ins} strand takes as input an *Insert-Listener($\triangle p_k$)* element that registers callbacks for new insertions in the p_k table. Upon insertion of a new tuple t_k into the p_k table, the *Insert-Listener* element outputs the new tuple, which is then used to perform a series of joins with the other input tables in its rule strand to derive new p tuples. Each newly derived p tuple is then passed to a *Project($\triangle p$)*, and then sent out via the *Network-Out elements*[2]. Each $RS1_{ins}$ strand takes as input new p tuples that arrives via the network, and inserts these tuples into its local p table using the *Insert($\triangle p$)* element.

Algorithm 4.4 Rule strands generation for incremental deletion of hard-state SN delta rules.

for each kth **delta rule** $\triangle p : - p_1, p_2, ..., \triangle p_k, ..., p_n, b_1, b_2, ..., b_m$
    $RS_{del} \leftarrow addElement(NULL, Delete\text{-}Listener(\triangle p_{k,del}))$
    for each derived predicate p_j **where** $j \neq k$
        $RS_{del} \leftarrow addElement(RS_{del}, Join(p_j))$
    end
    for each base predicate b_j
        $RS_{del} \leftarrow addElement(RS_{del}, Join(b_j))$
    end
    $RS_{del} \leftarrow addElement(RS_{del}, Project(\triangle p_{del})$
    $RS_{del} \leftarrow addElement(RS_{del}, Network\text{-}Out)$
    $RS1_{del} \leftarrow addElement(NULL, Network\text{-}In(\triangle p_{del}))$
    $RS1_{del} \leftarrow addElement(RS1_{del}, Delete(\triangle p))$
end

The RS_{del} and $RS1_{del}$ strands in Algorithm 4.4 are generated in a similar fashion for incremental deletions. The RS_{del} strand take as input tuples from a *Delete-Listener($\triangle p_{k,del}$)* element that outputs p_{del} tuples that have been deleted from the p_k table. The $RS1_{del}$ strand receives these tuples, and then delete those with the same values from the local p table using the *Delete($\triangle p$)* element.

Figure 4.5 shows an example of compiled dataflow with rule strands for the delta rules sp2a, sp2b-1 and sp2b-2 that we presented earlier in Section 4.2. For each delta rule, applying Algorithms 4.3 and 4.4 result in several strands for incremental insertions and deletions. These are denoted by strand labels with subscripts *ins* and *del*, respectively, in Figure 4.5. For example, strands sp2a$_{ins}$@S and sp2a$_{del}$@S are generated from the delta rule sp2a, and used to implement the incre-

---

[2]Note that outbound p tuples generated by RS_{ins} that are destined for local consumption are "wrapped around" to the *Network-In* element as input to $RS1_{ins}$ of the same dataflow locally, as described in Section 3.2.

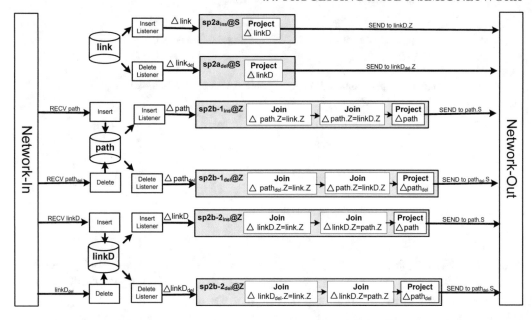

Figure 4.5: Rule strands for the SN delta rules sp2a, sp2b-1 and sp2b-2 with incremental maintenance.

mental recomputation of linkD table based on modifications to the link table. Similarly, strands $sp2b-1_{ins}@S$ and $sp2b-1_{del}@S$ are generated from delta rule sp2b-1, and strands $sp2b-2_{ins}@S$ and $sp2b-2_{del}@S$ are generated from delta rule sp2b-2.

In handling rules with aggregates, we apply techniques for incremental computation of aggregates [Ramakrishnan et al., 1992] in the presence of updates. The arrival of new tuples may invalidate existing aggregates, and incremental recomputations can be cheaper than computing the entire aggregate from scratch. For example, the re-evaluation costs for MIN and MAX aggregates are shown to be $O(\log n)$ time and $O(n)$ space [Ramakrishnan et al., 1992].

4.4.2   CENTRALIZED EXECUTION SEMANTICS

Before considering the distributed execution semantics of NDlog programs, we first provide an intuitive example for the centralized case. Figure 4.6 shows a *derivation tree* for path(@e,d,a,[e,a,b,d],7) based on the *Shortest-Path* program. The leaves in the tree are the link base tuples. The root and the intermediate nodes are tuples recursively derived from the children inputs by applying either rules sp1 and sp2. When updates occur to the base tuples, changes are propagated up the tree to the root. The left diagram shows updating the tree due to a change in base tuple link(@a,b,5), and the right diagram shows the deletion of link(@b,e,1).

For example, when the cost of link(@a,b,5) is updated from 5 to 1, there is a deletion of link(@a,b,5) followed by an insertion of link(@a,b,1). This in turn results in the dele-

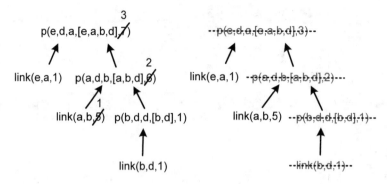

Figure 4.6: Derivation tree for derived `path` tuple from a to e.

tion of `path(@a,d,b,[a,b,d],6)` and `path(@e,d,a,[e,a,b,d],7)`, followed by the derivation of `path(@a,d,b,[a,b,d],2)` and `path(@e,d,a,[e,a,b,d],3)`. Similarly, the deletion of
`link(@b,d,1)` leads to the deletion of `path(@b,d,d,[b,d],1)`, `path(@a,d,b,[a,b,d],2)`,
and then `path(@e,d,a,[e,a,b,d],3)`.

Let FP_p be the set of tuples derived using PSN under the bursty model, and FFP_p be the set
of tuples that would be computed by PSN if starting from the quiesced state. The following theorem
holds [Loo, 2006].

Theorem (correctness): $FP_p = FFP_p$ *in a centralized setting.*

The proof requires that all changes (inserts, deletes, updates) are applied in the same order in
which they arrive. This is guaranteed by the FIFO queue of PSN and the use of timestamps.

4.4.3 DISTRIBUTED EXECUTION SEMANTICS

In order for incremental evaluation to work in a distributed environment, it is essential that along any
link in the network, there is a FIFO ordering of messages. That is, along any link literal `link(s,d)`,
facts derived at node s should arrive at node d in the same order in which they are derived (and vice
versa). This guarantees that updates can be applied in order. Using the same definition of FP_p and
FFP_p as before, assuming the link FIFO ordering, the following theorem holds:

Theorem (distributed correctness): $FP_p = FFP_p$ *in a distributed setting with FIFO links.*

As a refinement to the basic count algorithm, each derived tuple can be shipped with a compact
form of data provenance encoded using binary decision diagrams [Liu et al., 2009b]. With further
enhancement [Nigam et al., 2011], it is shown, with detailed formal proofs, that the provenance-
based approach ensures correctness even in the presence of message reordering in the network (i.e., no
FIFO ordering requirement).

4.5   PROCESSING SOFT-STATE RULES

Up to this point in the chapter, we have focused on the processing of *hard-state rules*. In this section, we build upon the earlier techniques to process *soft-state rules*. Recall from Section 2.4 that a rule is considered soft-state if it contains at least one soft-state predicate in the rule head or body.

Soft-state relations are stored in *soft-state tables* within the DN engine as described in Section 3.3. Unlike hard-state tables, these tables store tuples only for their specified lifetimes and expire them in a manner consistent with traditional soft-state semantics. Timeouts can be managed lazily in soft-state tables by purging any expired soft-state tuples whenever tables are accessed. Unlike hard-state tables, these soft-state tables do not require maintaining a derivation count for each unique tuple. Instead, soft-state tuples that are inserted into their respective tables will extend the lifetime of identical tuples.

Algorithm 4.5 Rule strands generation for incremental refresh of soft-state delta rules.

---

for each delta rule $\triangle p : - p_1, p_2, ..., \triangle p_k, ..., p_n, b_1, b_2, ..., b_m$
    $RS_{ref} \leftarrow addElement(NULL, Refresh\text{-}Listener(\triangle p_{k,ref}))$
    for each derived predicate p_j where $j \neq k$
        $RS_{ref} \leftarrow addElement(RS_{ref}, Join(p_j))$
    end
    for each base predicate b_j
        $RS_{ref} \leftarrow addElement(RS_{ref}, Join(b_j))$
    end
    $RS_{ref} \leftarrow addElement(RS_{ref}, Project(\triangle p)$
    if $(p.loc = p_k.loc)$
      then $RS_{ins} \leftarrow addElement(RS_{ins}, Insert(\triangle p))$
      else
          $RS_{ref} \leftarrow addElement(RS_{ref}, Network\text{-}Out)$
          $RS1_{ref} \leftarrow addElement(NULL, Network\text{-}In(\triangle p))$
          $RS1_{ref} \leftarrow addElement(RS1_{ref}, Insert(\triangle p))$
      end
    end
end

Prior to applying the SN rewrite, the processing of soft-state rules requires the same *localization rewrite* step described in Section 4.2. After localization, the SN rewrite is applied to all soft-state rules. Consider a soft-state rule of the form:

$$p : - s_1, s_2, ...s_m, h_1, h_2, ..., h_n, b_1, b_2, ...b_o \qquad (4.6)$$

where $s_1, s_2, ..., s_m$ are m soft-state derived predicates, $h_1, h_2, ..., h_n$ are n hard-state derived predicates, and $b_1, b_2, ..., b_o$ are o base predicates. The SN rewrite generates $m + n$ delta rules, one for each soft-state and hard-state derived predicate, where the kth *soft-state delta rule* takes as input $\triangle s_k$ tuples:

$$\triangle p : - s_1, s_2, ..., \triangle s_k, ..., s_m, h_1, h_2, ..., h_n, b_1, b_2, ...b_o. \qquad (4.7)$$

In addition, the jth *hard-state delta rule* takes as input $\triangle h_j$ tuples:

$$\triangle p : - s_1, ..., s_k, ..., s_m, h_1, h_2, ..., \triangle h_j, ..., h_n, b_1, b_2, ..., b_o. \qquad (4.8)$$

Following the generation of delta rules, Algorithm 4.3 is used to generate the strands for incremental insertions in a similar fashion as hard-state rules. However, instead of using Algorithm 4.4 for generating strands for incremental deletions, Algorithm 4.5 is used to generate strands for *incremental refreshes*. The difference is due to soft-state rules being incrementally maintained using *cascaded refreshes* instead of *cascaded deletions* (see Section 2.4). In Algorithm 4.3, the strand RS_{ref} takes as input a *Refresh-Listener($\triangle p_{k,ref}$)* element that outputs soft-state p_k tuples that have been refreshed. These p_k tuples are then used to derive p tuples, which are then inserted by the $RS1_{ref}$ into local p tables. If p is a soft-state relation, these new insertions will lead to further refreshes being generated, hence achieving cascaded refreshes.

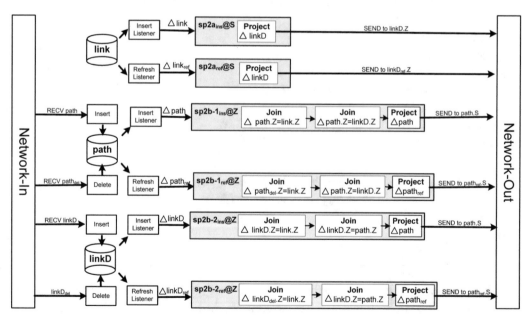

Figure 4.7: Rule strands for distributed soft-state management of delta rules sp2a, sp2b-1 and sb2b-2.

For completeness, Figure 4.7 shows an example dataflow for a soft-state version of rule sp2, assuming that link and path have been declared as soft-state relations. In contrast to Figure 4.5, *Refresh-Listener* elements are used instead of *Delete-Listener* elements to generate soft-state refreshes.

4.5.1   EVENT SOFT-STATE RULES

Having presented the general steps required to process soft-state rules, in this section we focus on a special-case soft-state rule: the *event soft-state rule* presented in Section 2.4. As a quick recap, an event soft-state rule is of the form:

$$p :- e, p_1, p_2, ..., p_n, b_1, b_2, ..., b_m. \tag{4.9}$$

The rule body consists of one event predicate e; the other predicates $p, p_1, p_2, ..., p_n$ can either soft- or hard-state predicates, and $b_1, b_2, ..., b_m$ are base predicates as before.

The dataflow generation for event soft-state rules is simplified due to the fact that events are not materialized. As we discussed in Section 2.4.2, NDlog's event model does not permit two events to coincide in time. Hence, a rule with more than one event table would never produce any output. The only delta rule that generates any output tuples is the *event delta rule* that takes as input new e event tuples of the form:

$$\triangle p :- \triangle e, p_1, p_2, ..., p_n, b_1, b_2, b_m. \tag{4.10}$$

Since the delta predicate (prepended with $\triangle$) is essentially a stream of update events, none of the other delta rules generates any output and we can exclude them from dataflow generation.

```
pp1 ping(@S,D,E) :- periodic(@S,E,5), link(@S,D).
pp2 pingMsg(S,@D,E) :- ping(@S,D,E), link(@S,D).
```

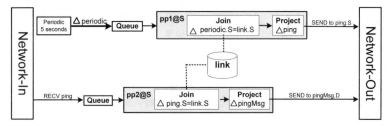

Figure 4.8: Rule strands for event soft-state rules pp1 and pp2.

Figure 4.8 shows the execution plan for rules pp1 and pp2 from the *Ping-Pong* program from Chapter 2. The first strand pp1@S takes as input a *Periodic* element that generates a periodic(@S,E,5) tuple every 5 s at node S with random event identifier E. This tuple is then used to join with link tuples to generate a ping event tuple that is then used in strand pp2@S to generate pingMsg event tuples.

The output of event soft-state rules can also be an aggregate computation, which is done on a *per-event* basis. Examples of such aggregate computations are shown in rules 12 and 13 from the declarative Chord specifications in Chapter 6. These rules compute aggregate MIN values stored in bestLookupDist and lookup tuples respectively, one for each input event.

l2 bestLookupDist(@NI,K,R,E,MIN<D>) :- nodeID(@NI,N),
                        lookup(@NI,K,R,E), finger(@NI,I,B,BI),
                        D = K - B - 1, B in (N,K).

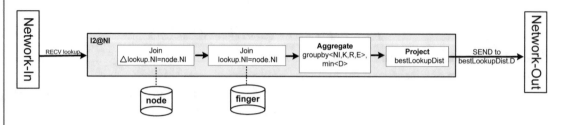

Figure 4.9: Rule strand for rule l2, an event soft-state rule with aggregation.

Figure 4.9 shows the strand l2@NI generated for rule l2. This strand takes as input new
lookup event tuples, which are then executed within the strand by joining with the node and
finger tables to generate a set of matching output tuples. These output tuples are then used by the
Aggregate element to compute a bestLookupDist tuple that stores the computed MIN value. Note
that in this case, we have additional runtime checks in place in the dataflow execution to ensure that
each lookup tuple is executed in its entirety within the strand to generate the bestLookupDist
tuple before the strand processes the next lookup tuple.

4.6   SUMMARY

In this chapter, we described how NDlog programs can be processed by generating distributed
dataflows. We first demonstrated how traditional semi-naïve evaluation for centralized Datalog
programs can be realized in our system, and further extend the techniques to handle distributed and
soft-state NDlog rules. We further showed how we can ensure correct semantics of long-running
NDlog programs in dynamic networks for both hard-state and soft-state rules. In the next chapter,
we present the use of NDlog to express more complex overlay networks.

CHAPTER 5

Declarative Routing

Having given an overview of the NDlog language, this chapter focuses on *declarative routing*: the declarative specification of routing protocols for building extensible routing infrastructures. Declarative networking aims to strike a better balance between the extensibility and the robustness of a routing infrastructure. In addition to being a concise and flexible language for routing protocols, NDlog is amenable to static analysis, making it an attractive language for building safe, extensible routing infrastructures.

The chapter is organized as follows. First, Section 5.1 presents the motivation of declarative routing. Next, Section 5.2 provides an overview of declarative routing's execution model. Section 5.3 illustrates the flexibility of NDlog through several declarative routing examples. The challenges of security are addressed in Section 5.4, and route maintenance under dynamic networks in Section 5.5. Finally, evaluation results are presented in Section 5.6.

5.1   MOTIVATION

Designing routing protocols is a difficult process. This is not only because of the distributed nature and scale of the networks, but also because of the need to balance the extensibility and flexibility of these protocols on one hand, and their robustness and efficiency on the other hand. One need look no further than the Internet for an illustration of these different tradeoffs.

Today's Internet routing protocols, while arguably robust and efficient, are hard to change to accommodate the needs of new applications such as improved resilience and higher throughput. Upgrading even a single router is hard [Handley et al., 2005]. Getting a distributed routing protocol implemented correctly is even harder. And in order to change or upgrade a deployed routing protocol, one must get access to *each* router to modify its software. This process is made even more tedious and error prone by the use of conventional programming languages that were not designed with networking in mind.

Several solutions have been proposed to address the lack of flexibility and extensibility in Internet routing. Overlay networks allow third parties to replace Internet routing with new, "from-scratch" implementations of routing functionality that run at the application layer. However, overlay networks simply move the problem from the network to the application layer where third parties have control: implementing or updating an overlay routing protocol still requires a complete protocol design and implementation, and requires access to the overlay nodes.

On the other hand, a radically different approach, *active networks* [Tennenhouse et al., 1997], allows network packets to modify the operation of networks by allowing routers to execute code within active network packets. This allows new functionality to be introduced to existing active networks without the need to have direct access to routers. However, due to the general programming models proposed for active networks, they present difficulties in both performance and the security and reliability of the resulting infrastructure.

Declarative routing provides a new point in this design space that aims to strike a better balance between the extensibility and the robustness of a routing infrastructure. With declarative routing, a routing protocol is implemented by writing a simple NDlog program, which is then executed in a distributed fashion at some or all of the nodes. Declarative routing can be viewed as a safer instantiation of active networks which aims to balance the concerns of expressiveness, performance and security, properties which are needed for an extensible routing infrastructure to succeed.

Declarative routing could evolve to be used in a variety of ways. One extreme view of the future of routing is that individual end-users (or their applications) will explicitly request routes with particular properties, by submitting the NDlog programs for route construction to the network. The safety and simplicity of declarative specifications would clearly be beneficial in that context. A more incremental view is that an administrator at an ISP might reconfigure the ISP's routers by issuing an NDlog program to the network; different NDlog programs would allow the administrator to easily implement various routing policies between different nodes or different traffic classes. Even in this managed scenario, the simplicity and safety of declarative routing has benefits over the current relatively fragile approaches to upgrading routers. While this second scenario is arguably the more realistic one, declarative networking allows the other extreme in which any node (including end-hosts) can issue an NDlog program. We take this extreme position in order to explore the limits of the design.

5.2   EXECUTION MODEL

The routing infrastructure is modelled as a directed graph, where each link is associated with a set of parameters (e.g., loss rate, available bandwidth, delay). The router nodes in the routing infrastructure can either be IP routers or overlay nodes.

Figure 5.1 shows the architecture of a typical declarative router. Like a traditional router, a declarative router maintains a *neighbor table*, which contains the set of neighbor routers that this router can forward messages to, and a *forwarding table* in the *forwarding plane*, that is used to route incoming packets based on their destination addresses to neighboring nodes along a computed path.

The forwarding table is created by the routing protocol that executes on the *control plane* of each router. Each routing protocol takes as input any updates to the local neighbor table, and implements a distributed computation where routers exchange route information with neighboring routers to compute new routes.

In a declarative router, a declarative networking (DN) runtime engine runs on the control plane and takes as input local routing information such as the neighbor table. Instead of running a single routing protocol, the DN engine allows any routing protocols expressed in NDlog to be executed in a distributed fashion in the network. The results of the program are used to establish router forwarding

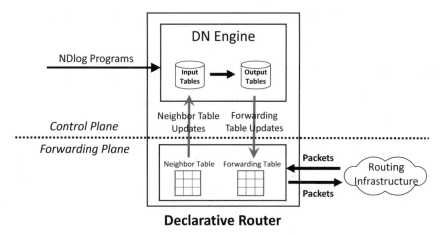

Figure 5.1: A declarative router.

state which the routers use for forwarding data packets. Alternatively, the computed results can be sent back to the party that issued the NDlog program, which can use these results to perform source routing. Note that while the DN engine is used on the control plane in declarative routing, it can be used more generally on the forwarding plane as well, as Chapter 6 demonstrates.

NDlog program dissemination and execution can happen in a variety of ways. In static scenarios, the program may be "baked in" to another artifact – e.g., router firmware or peer-to-peer application software that is bundled with the DN engine. More flexibly, the program could be disseminated upon initial declaration to all or some of the nodes running the DN engine. It may be sufficient to perform dissemination via flooding, particularly if the program will be long-lived, amortizing the cost of the initial flood. As an optimization, instead of flooding the program in the network, one can instead "piggy-back" dissemination onto program execution: the program can be embedded into the first data tuple sent to each neighboring node as part of executing the NDlog program.

This execution model is based on a *fully distributed* implementation, where routes are computed in a decentralized fashion. As an alternative, in a *centralized* design such as the Routing Control Platform [Feamster et al., 2004], network information is periodically gathered from the routing infrastructure, and stored at one or more central servers. Each program is sent to one or more of these servers, which process the programs using their internal databases and set up the forwarding state at the routers in the network.

During the execution of NDlog program, the neighbor table is periodically updated in response to link failures, new links, or link metric changes. These updates are performed by the routers themselves using standard mechanisms such as periodic pings. The DN engine is then notified of updates to the neighbor table, and will incrementally recompute entries into the forwarding table.

In declarative routing, this simple interface is the only interaction required between the DN engine and the router's core forwarding logic.

5.3   ROUTING PROTOCOLS BY EXAMPLES

To highlight the flexibility of NDlog, several examples of useful routing protocols expressed as NDlog rules are provided. These examples range from well-known routing protocols (distance vector, dynamic source routing, multicast, etc.) to higher-level routing concepts such as QoS constraints. This is by no means intended to be an exhaustive coverage of the possibilities of declarative routing protocols. The main goal here is to illustrate the natural connection between recursive programs and network routing, and to highlight the flexibility, ease of programming, and ease of reuse afforded by a declarative language. Routing protocols can be expressed in a few NDlog rules, and additional protocols can be created by simple modifications.

5.3.1   BEST-PATH ROUTING

Consider the base rules sp1 and sp2 used in the first *Shortest-Path* program from the previous chapter. That example computes *all-pairs shortest paths*. In practice, a more common program would compute *all-pairs best paths*. By modifying rules sp2, sp3 and sp4, the *Best-Path* program in Figure 5.2 generalizes the all-pairs shortest paths computation, and computes the best paths for any path metric C:

```
bp1 path(@S,D,D,P,C) :- link(@S,D,C), P=f_init(S,D).
bp2 path(@S,D,Z,P,C) :- link(@S,Z,C1), path(@Z,D,Z2,P2,C2),
                        C = f_compute(C1,C2), P = f_concatPath(S,P2).
bp3 bestPathCost(@S,D,AGG<C>) :- path(@S,D,Z,P,C).
bp4 bestPath(@S,D,P,C) :- bestPathCost(@S,D,C), path(@S,D,Z,P,C).
Query bestPath(@S,D,P,C).
```

Figure 5.2: Best-Path program.

The aggregation function (AGG) is left unspecified. By changing AGG and the function f_compute used for computing the path cost C, the *Best-Path* program can generate best paths based on any metric including link latency, available bandwidth and node load. For example, if the program is used for computing the shortest paths, f_sum is the appropriate instantiation for f_compute in rule bpr1, and MIN is the instantiation for AGG. The resulting bestPath tuples are stored at the source nodes, and are used by end-hosts to perform source routing. Instead of computing the best path between any two nodes, this program can be easily modified to compute *all* paths, *any* path or the *Best-k* paths between any two nodes.

To avoid generating path cycles, an extra predicate f_inPath(P2,S)=false can be added to rule bp2 to avoid computing best paths with cycles (e.g., when computing the longest latency paths). The rules from the *Best-Path* program can be further extended by including constraints that enforce a QoS requirement specified by end-hosts. For example, one can restrict the set of paths to those with costs below a loss or latency threshold k by adding an extra constraint C<k to the rules computing `path`.

5.3.2   DISTANCE-VECTOR ROUTING

dv1 hop(@S,D,D,C) :- link(@S,D,C).
dv2 hop(@S,D,Z,C) :- link(@S,Z,C1), hop(@Z,D,W,C2), C = f_compute(C1,C2).
dv3 bestHopCost(@S,D,AGG<C>) :- hop(@S,D,Z,C).
dv4 bestPathHop(@S,D,Z,C) :- hop(@S,D,Z,C),bestHopCost(@S,D,C).
Query bestPathHop(@S,D,Z,C).

Figure 5.3: Distance-Vector program.

Figure 5.3 shows a program that expresses the distance vector protocol for customized best routes for any given path metric. Rules `dv1` and `dv2` are modified from rules `bp1` and `bp2` from the previous example to generate the `hop` tuple that maintains only the next hop on the path, and not the entire path vector P itself[1]. Rules `dv3` and `dv4` are added to set up routing state in the network: *bestPathHop(@S,D,Z,C)* is stored at node S, where Z is the next hop on the best path to node D.

The distance vector protocol has the count-to-infinity problem [Peterson and Davie, 2007], where link failures may result in long (sometimes infinite) protocol convergence times. By making a modification to rule `dv2` and adding rule `dv5`, the well-known *split-horizon with poison reverse* [Peterson and Davie, 2007] fix to this problem can be applied as follows.

#include(dv1,dv3,dv4)
dv2 hop(@S,D,Z,C) :- link(@S,Z,C1), hop(@Z,D,W,C2), C = C1 + C2, W != S.
dv5 hop(@S,D,Z,infinity):- link(@S,Z,C1), hop(@Z,D,S,C2).
Query bestPathHop(@S,D,Z,C).

Figure 5.4: Distance-Vector program with count-to-infinity fix in NDlog.

`#include` is a macro used to include earlier rules. Rule `dv2` expresses that if node Z learns about the path to D from node S, then node Z does not report this path back to S. Rule `dv5` expresses that if node Z receives a path tuple with destination D from node S, then node Z will send a path with destination D and infinite cost to node S. This ensures that eventually node S will not use Z to get to D.

---

[1]The W field in `dv2` represents the next-hop to node D from intermediate node Z, and can be ignored by node S in computing its next hop to node D.

5.3.3   POLICY-BASED ROUTING

The previous examples all illustrate a typical network-wide routing policy. To restrict the scope of routing, e.g., by precluding paths that involve "undesirable" nodes. An example would be finding a path among nodes in an overlay network on PlanetLab that avoids nodes belonging to untruthful or flaky ISPs. Such policy constraints can be simply expressed by adding an additional rule.

#include(bp1,bp2)
pbr1 permitPath(@S,D,Z,P,C) :- path(@S,D,Z,P,C),
                                 excludeNode(@S,W), f_inPath(P,W)=false.
Query permitPath(@S,D,P,C).

Figure 5.5: Policy-based routing program.

    In this program, an additional table `excludeNode` is introduced, where `excludeNode(@S,W)` is a tuple that represents the fact that node S does not carry any traffic for node W. This table is stored at each node S.

    If rules `bp1` and `bp2` are included as rules, `bestPath` tuples can be generated to meet the above policy. Other policy based decisions include ignoring the paths reported by selected nodes or insisting that some paths have to pass through (or avoid) one or multiple pre-determined set of nodes.

5.3.4   DYNAMIC SOURCE ROUTING

All of the previous examples use what is called *right* recursion, since the recursive predicates (e.g., `path` in the rules sp2, bp2 and dv2) appears to the right of the matching `link`. Given that predicates are executed in a left-to-right order, the program semantics do not change if the order of `path` and `link` in the body of these rules are flipped, but the execution strategy does change. In fact, the Dynamic Source Routing (DSR) protocol [Johnson and Maltz, 1996] can be implemented by using *left recursion* as follows.

#include(bp1,bp3,bp4)
dsr2 path(@S,D,Z,P,C) :- path(@S,Z,W,P1,C1), link(@Z,D,C2),
                               C = f_compute(C1,C2), P = f_concatPath(P1,D).
Query bestPath(@S,D,P,C).

Figure 5.6: Dynamic Source Routing program.

    Rule `bp1` produces new one-hop paths from existing link tuples as before. Rule `dsr2` matches the destination fields of newly computed path tuples with the source fields of link tuples. This requires newly computed path tuples be shipped by their destination fields to find matching links, hence ensuring that each source node will recursively follow the links along all reachable paths. Here, the function `f_concatPath(P,D)` returns a new path vector with node D appended to P. These rules can also be used in combination with bpr1 and bpr2 to generate the best paths. By adding two extra rules not shown here, the logic for sending each path on the reverse path from the destination to the source node can be expressed.

5.3.5 LINK STATE

To further illustrate the flexibility of this approach, consider a link-state protocol that moves route information around the network very differently from the best-path variants. The *Link-State* program, found in Figure 5.7, expresses the flooding of links to all nodes in the network.

```
ls1 floodLink(@S,S,D,C,S) :- link(@S,D,C).
ls2 floodLink(@M,S,D,C,N) :- link(@N,M,C1), floodLink(@N,S,D,C,W), M != W.
Query floodLink(@M,S,D,C,N)
```

Figure 5.7: Link-State program.

`floodLink(@M,S,D,C,N)` is a tuple storing information about `link(@S,D,C)`. This tuple is flooded in the network starting from source node S. During the flooding process, node M is the current node it is flooded to, while node N is the node that forwarded this tuple to node M.

Rule `ls1` generates a `floodLink` tuple for every link at each node. Rule `ls2` states that each node N that receives a `floodLink` tuple recursively forwards the tuple to all neighbors M except the node W that it received the tuple from. NDlog is based on the relational model that utilizes set computations, where duplicate tuples are not considered for computation twice. This ensures that no similar `floodLink` tuple is forwarded twice.

Once all the links are available at each node, a local version of the *Best-Path* program in Figure 5.2 is then executed locally using the `floodLink` tuples to generate all the best paths.

5.3.6 MULTICAST

The examples given so far support protocols for unicast routing. As a more complex example, NDlog is used to construct a multicast dissemination tree from a designated root node to multiple destination nodes that "subscribe" to the multicast group. The following *Source-Specific-Multicast* program sets up such a forwarding tree rooted at a source node *a* for group *gid*:

For simplicity of exposition, this program utilizes the *Best-Path* program (rules bp1, bp2, bp3, bp4) to compute the all-pairs best paths. We will discuss program optimization techniques to reduce the communication overhead for small multicast groups in Section 7.1.2.

Each destination node *n* joins the group *gid* with source *a* by issuing the program *join-Group(@n,a,gid)*. This results in the generation of the following derived tuples.

- **joinMessage(@nodeID, prevNodeID, pathVector, source, gid)**. This tuple stores the multicast *join* message for group *gid*. It is sent by every destination node along its best path to

```
#include(bp1,bp2,bp3,bp4)
m1 joinMessage(@I,N,P,S,G) :- joinGroup(@N,S,G), bestPath(@N,S,P1,C),
                       I = f_head(P1), P = f_tail(P1).
m2 joinMessage(@I,J,P,S,G) :- joinMessage(@J,K,P1,S,G), I = f_head(P1),
                       P = f_tail(P1), f_isEmpty(P1) = false.
m3 forwardState(@I,J,S,G) :- joinMessage(@I,J,P,S,G).
Query joinGroup(@N,a,gid)
```

Figure 5.8: Source-Specific-Multicast program.

the *@source* address of the group. At each intermediate node with address *nodeID*, *prevNodeID* stores the address of the node that forwarded this tuple. *pathVector* is the remaining path that this message needs to traverse in order to reach the source node.

- **forwardState(@nodeID, forwardNodeID, source, gid).** This tuple represents source-specific state of the multicast dissemination tree at each intermediate node with address *nodeID*. If a message from *source* of multicast group *gid* is received at *nodeID*, it is forwarded to *forwardNodeID*.

Rules m1 and m2 create the `joinMessage` tuple at each participating destination node N, and forward this tuple along the best path to the source node S. Upon receiving a `joinMessage` tuple, rule M3 allows each intermediate node *I* to set up the forwarding state using the `forwardState(@I,J,S,G)` tuple. The predicate function `f_head(P)` returns the next node in the path vector P, and `f_tail(P)` returns the path vector P with the first node removed. `f_isEmpty(P)` returns true if P is empty.

Instead of a *source-specific* tree, with minor modifications, we can construct *core-based trees* [Ballardie et al., 1993]. Here, each participating node sends a *join* message to a designated *core* node to build a *shared* tree rooted at the core. Messages are then unicast to the core, which disseminates it using the shared tree.

5.4   SECURITY ISSUES

Security is a key concern with any extensible system [Bershad et al., 1995, Stonebraker, 1986]. In the network domain, this concern is best illustrated by active networks which, at the extreme, allow routers to download and execute arbitrary code.

Declarative routing's approach essentially proposes NDlog as a Domain Specific Language (DSL) [van Deursen et al., 2000] for programming the control plane of a network. DSLs typically provide security benefits by having restricted expressivity. NDlog is attractive in this respect, both because of its strong theoretical foundations, and its practical aspects. NDlog rules written in the core[2] Datalog language have polynomial time and space complexities in the size of the in-

---

[2]Such a "core" language does not contain predicates constructed using function symbols.

put [Abiteboul et al., 1995]. This property provides a natural bound on the resource consumption of NDlog programs.

However, many implementations of Datalog (including NDlog) augment the core language with various functions. Example of such functions are boolean predicates, arithmetic functions, and string or list manipulation logic (e.g., `f_init`, `f_concatPath`, `f_inPath`, `f_isEmpty`, `f_head` and `f_tail`). With the addition of arbitrary functions, the time complexity of a NDlog program is no longer polynomial.

Fortunately, several powerful static tests have been developed to check for the termination of an augmented Datalog program on a given input [Krishnamurthy et al., 1996]. In a nutshell, these tests identify recursive definitions in the program rules, and check whether these definitions terminate. Examples of recursive definitions that terminate are ones that evaluate monotonically increasing/decreasing predicates whose values are upper/lower bounded.

The NDlog rules that pass these checks are general enough to express a large class of routing protocols. Thus, the NDlog language offers a good balance between expressiveness and safety. All the examples presented in this chapter pass such termination tests.

In addition, the execution of the program is "sandboxed" within the program engine. These properties prevent the program from accessing arbitrary router state such as in-flight messages, and the router's operating system state. As a result, NDlog eliminates many of the risks usually associated with extensible systems.

Of course, there are many other security issues beyond the safety of the NDlog language. Two examples are denial-of-service attacks and compromised routers. These problems are orthogonal to network extensibility, and are not directly addressed in this chapter.

5.5   ROUTE MAINTENANCE

During program execution, changes in the network might result in some of the computed routes becoming stale. These can be caused by link failures, or changes in the link metrics when these metrics are used in route computation. Ideally, the program should rapidly recompute a new route, especially in the case of link failures.

One solution is to simply recompute the programs from scratch, either periodically or driven by the party that has issued the programs. However, recomputing the program from scratch is expensive, and if done only periodically, the time to react to failures is a half-period on average.

The approach employed in declarative networking is to utilize long-running or *continuous* queries that incrementally recompute new results based on changes in the network. To ensure incremental recomputations, all intermediate states of each program are retained in the program processor until the program is no longer required. The intermediate states include any shipped tuples used in join computation, and any intermediate derived tuples.

As discussed in Section 5.2, each declarative router is responsible for detecting changes to its local information or base tables and reporting these changes to its local program processor. These base tuple updates result in the addition of tuples into base tables, or the replacement of existing base tuples that have the same unique key as the update tuples. The continuous queries then utilize these updates and the intermediate state of rule executions to incrementally recompute some of their derived tuples.

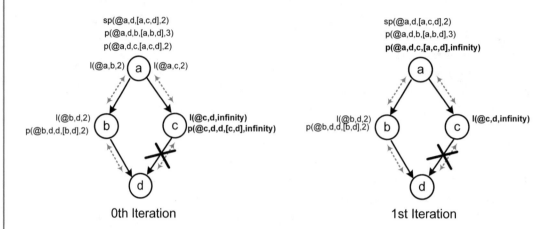

Figure 5.9: Derivation of alternative shortest path from node *a* to d when link(@a,b,1) is deleted.

To illustrate, consider the *Shortest-Path* program that we introduce in Chapter 2. Figure 5.9 shows a simple four node network where all four nodes are running the *Shortest-Path* program. l(@S,D,C), p(@S,D,Z,P,C) and sp(@S,D,P,C) abbreviates link(@S,D,C), path(@S,D,Z,P,C) and shortestPath(@S,D,P,C) respectively.

Prior to the link failure, assuming that all shortest paths between all pairs have been computed, the figure shows the changes to the intermediate program states that led to the derivation of a new shortest path from node a to d when node d fails. For simplicity, only the derived paths along the solid lines are shown, even though the network connectivity is bidirectional (dashed lines). An invalid path is denoted as one with infinite cost, although in practice, they are deleted from the path table. When l(@c,d,1) is deleted, the following steps are taken to derive sp(@a,d,[a,b,d],3):

1. When neighbor c detects the failure of its link to d via a timeout, it generates an updated base tuple l(@c,d,∞) locally. This replaces the previous tuple l(@c,d,1).

2. All one-hop paths at node c that traverse through d are set to infinite costs. For example, node c generates p(@c,d,d,[c,d],∞).

3. p(@c,d,d,[c,d],∞) is joined with l(@a,c,1) to produce p(@a,d,c,[a,c,d],∞) which is sent to node a.

4. Upon receiving p(@a,d,c[a,c,d],∞), node a computes a new shortest path sp(@a,d,[a,b,d],3).

In this example, since the entire path vector is computed, one can check for potential cycles. The failure is propagated hop-by-hop. Hence, the time taken for any update to converge is proportional to the network diameter, and bounded by the time it takes for a program to be executed from scratch.

Updates to link costs are handled in a similar fashion, except that rather than setting the costs to infinity, they are recomputed based on the new link costs. The updated paths may trigger further computation. For example, when the cost of paths are changed, rules bpr1 and bpr2 of the *Best-Path* program will generate alternative best paths accordingly.

Chapter 4 revisits in detail the processing of continuous queries using both hard-state and soft-state incremental view maintenance techniques [Gupta et al., 1993].

5.6   EVALUATION

This section presents the performance evaluation of declarative routing protocols written in NDlog using P2 [P2]. The main metrics used in the evaluation are the following.

Convergence time: Given a quiesced network, the time taken for the network protocol to generate all its eventual network state. This is equivalent to achieving *fixpoint* during NDlog program execution, where there are no new derivations from all rules that are being executed.

Communication overhead: The number of bytes transferred for each network protocol in order to achieve convergence in a quiesced network. The experiment considers both aggregate communication overhead (MB), as well as per-node bandwidth (KBps).

As the input, network topologies are generated by GT-ITM [GT-ITM] (using the transit-stub configuration), a package that is widely used to model Internet topologies. A topology has four transit nodes, eight nodes per stub and three stubs per transit node. Latency between transit nodes is 50 ms, latency between transit nodes and their stub nodes is 10 ms, and latency between any two nodes in the same stub is 2 ms. The link capacity is set to 10 Mbps. Given the small size of the network, the topology is limited to four transit domains.

The declarative routing protocol runs as an overlay network over the base GT-ITM topology where each overlay node is assigned to one of the stub nodes. Each overlay node runs the P2 engine on one machine, and picks four randomly selected overlay neighbors which are stored as facts in each local `link` table.

5.6.1   SCALABILITY OF PATH-VECTOR PROTOCOL

The first experiment measures the performance of the system when all nodes are running the *Shortest-Path* program of Chapter 2, which implements the path-vector protocol used to compute the shortest latency paths between all pairs of nodes. The implementation uses the *aggregate selections* optimization to avoid sending redundant path tuples (Section 7.1.1), where the most recently computed shortest paths are batched and sent to neighboring nodes every 500 ms. The duration of 500 ms is chosen as it is an upper bound on the latency between any two nodes. This ensures that computed paths

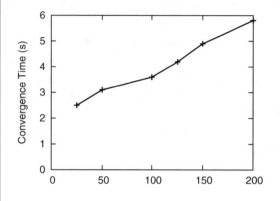

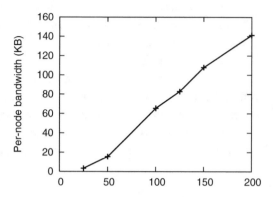

Figure 5.10: Convergence latency (s) vs. number of nodes.

Figure 5.11: Per-node communication overhead (KB).

at each iteration have sufficient time to be propagated and accumulated at every node for periodic aggregate selections to be most effective.

Figures 5.10 and 5.11 show the convergence latency and per-node communication overhead for the *Shortest-Path* program as the number of nodes increases from 25 to 200. The following wo observations are made.

- The convergence latency for the *Shortest-Path* program is proportional to the network diameter. This is expected because in a static network, the convergence time of the path vector protocol depends on the time taken to compute the *longest* shortest paths, which is bounded by the time taken for the computed shortest paths to propagate in the network (i.e., $500ms \times D_{hop}$, where D_{hop} is the network diameter in terms of hop count).

- The per-node communication overhead increases linearly with the number of nodes. This is because each node needs to compute the shortest path to every other node in the network.

Both these observations are consistent with the scalability properties of the traditional distance vector and path vector protocols, suggesting that declarative routing does not introduce any fundamental overheads when used to implement traditional routing protocols.

5.6.2 INCREMENTAL EVALUATION IN DYNAMIC NETWORKS

The next experiment examines the overhead of incrementally maintaining NDlog program results in a dynamic network. The same *Shortest-Path* program runs on 100 nodes over a period of time, and subject the network to bursty updates as described in Section 4.4. Each update burst involves randomly selecting 10% of all links, and then updating the cost metric by up to 10%.

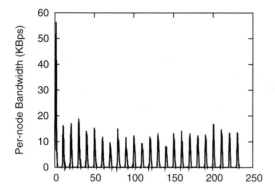

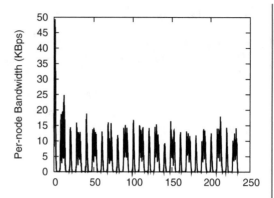

Figure 5.12: Per-node bandwidth (KBps) for peri-odic link updates on latency metric (10 s update interval).

Figure 5.13: Per-node bandwidth (KBps) for peri-odic link updates (interleaving 2 s and 8 s update interval).

The experiment adopts the shortest-path random metric, since executing the NDlog program using this metric is most demanding in terms of bandwidth usage and convergence time. This is because, as discussed in Section 7.1.1, aggregate selections are most useful for queries whose input tuples tend to arrive over the network out of order in terms of the monotonic aggregate – e.g., computing "shortest" paths for metrics that are not correlated with the network delays that dictate the arrival of the tuples during execution.

Figure 5.12 plots the per-node communication overhead, when applying a batch of updates every 10 s. Two points are worth noting. First, the time it takes the program to converge after a burst of updates is well within the convergence time of running the program from scratch. This is reflected in the communication overhead, which increases sharply after a burst of updates is applied, but then disappears long before the next burst of updates (Figure 5.12). Second, each burst peaks at 19 KBps, which is only 32% of the peak bandwidth and 28% of the aggregate bandwidth of the original computation. The results demonstrate the usefulness of performing incremental evaluation in response to changes in the network, as opposed to recomputing the queries from scratch

The experiment is repeated using a more demanding update workload (Figure 5.13), where update intervals of 2 s and 8 s are interleaved, the former interval being less than the from-scratch convergence time of 3.6 s. Despite the fact that bursts are sometimes occurring faster than queries can run, bandwidth usage is similar to the less demanding update workload, peaking at 24 KBps and converging within the from-scratch convergence time.

5.7   SUMMARY

This chapter motivates declarative routing, as a means to permit flexible routing over the Internet. Through several examples, we demonstrate that the NDlog language is natural for expressing a wide variety of network routing protocols. Interestingly, two important routing protocols (dynamic source routing and path vector protocols) differ only in the order in which predicates are evaluated. Section 5.6 measures the performance of declarative routing protocols such as the *Best-Path* program and validate that the scalability trends are similar to that of traditional approaches.

CHAPTER 6

Declarative Overlays

The previous chapter demonstrated the flexibility and compactness of NDlog for specifying a variety of routing protocols. In practice, most distributed systems are much more complex than simple routing protocols; in addition to routing, they typically also perform application-level message forwarding and handle the formation and maintenance of a network as well.

All large-scale distributed systems inherently use one or more application-level overlay networks as part of their operation. In some cases, the overlay is prominent: for example, file-sharing networks maintain neighbor tables to route queries. In other systems, the overlay or overlays may not be as explicit: for example, Microsoft Exchange email servers within an enterprise maintain an overlay network among themselves using a link-state algorithm over TCP for routing mail and status messages.

This chapter on *declarative overlays* demonstrates the use of NDlog to implement practical application-level overlay networks. In declarative overlays, applications submit to DN a concise NDlog program which describes an overlay network, and the DN system executes the program to maintain routing tables, perform neighbor discovery and provide forwarding for the overlay.

This chapter is organized as follows. Section 6.1 presents the execution model of declarative overlays. Two example NDlog programs are presented: the Narada [Chu et al., 2000] mesh for end-system multicast in Section 6.2, and the Chord [Stoica et al., 2001] distributed hash table in Section 6.3 respectively. Finally, evaluation results are shown in Section 6.4.

6.1   EXECUTION MODEL

A typical overlay network consists of three functionalities.

- **Routing** involves the computation and maintenance of routing tables at each node based on input neighbor tables. This functionality is typically known as the *control plane* of a network.

- **Forwarding** involves the delivery of overlay messages along the computed routes based on the destination addresses of the messages. This functionality is typically known as the *forwarding plane* of a network.

- **Overlay formation and maintenance** involves the process of joining an overlay network and maintaining the neighbor set at each node. The selected neighbors are used as input to the control plane for route computations.

In declarative routing presented in Chapter 5, NDlog programs are used solely for programming the control plane. Hence, all the previous routing examples consist of NDlog rules that compute routes based on input links. On the other hand, in declarative overlays, NDlog programs implement the additional functionalities of *forwarding* and *overlay formation and maintenance*. As examples later in this chapter will illustrate, these programs are more complex due to the handling of message delivery, acknowledgments, failure detection and timeouts required by the additional functionalities. Not surprisingly, the programs presented in this section utilize soft-state data and soft-state rules introduced in Chapter 2 extensively. Despite the increased complexity, the NDlog programs are significantly more compact compared to equivalent C++ implementations.

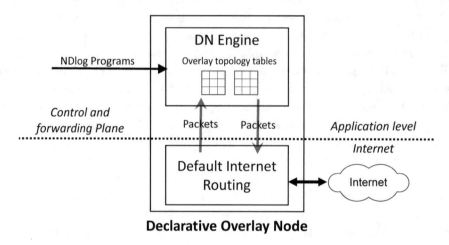

Figure 6.1: A Declarative Overlay Node.

Figure 6.1 illustrates the execution model of declarative overlays. The DN system resides at the application level, and all messages are routed via the default Internet routing. In addition, by using the default Internet for routing between overlay nodes at the application level, it is assumed that there is full connectivity in the underlying network. Every node participating in the overlay network can send a message to another node via the underlying network, and there is an entry in the link table for every source and destination pair of nodes.

6.2   NARADA MESH

To provide a simple but concrete example of a declarative overlay, we first present a popular overlay network for End System Multicast (ESM) called Narada [Chu et al., 2000]. A typical ESM overlay consists of two layers: the first layer constructs and maintains a mesh connecting all members in the group, while the second layer constructs delivery trees on top of the mesh using typical multicast algorithms such as the distance vector multicast protocol (DVMRP) [Deering and Cheriton, 1990] (see Sections 5.3.2 and 5.3.6 for examples on DVMRP). This section focuses on the first layer: constructing a Narada-like mesh here as an example of the use of NDlog.

Briefly, the mesh maintenance algorithm works as follows. Each node maintains a set of neighbors, and the set of all members in the group. Every member epidemically propagates keep-alive messages for itself, associated with a monotonically increasing sequence number. At the same time, neighbors exchange information about membership liveness and sequence numbers, ensuring that every member will eventually learn of all the other group members' liveness. If a member fails to hear from a direct neighbor for a period, it declares its neighbor dead, updating its own membership state and propagating this information to the rest of the population.

In addition, each node periodically probes a random group member to measuring the round-trip latency. Based on the measured round-trip latencies to all group members, each node selects a subset of the members to be its neighbors so that its predefined utility function is maximized. The rest of this section shows how the mesh maintenance portion of Narada can be expressed in NDlog. The definitions and initialization rules found in Figure 6.2 are used in Narada.

---

materialize(sequence, infinity, 1, keys(2)).
materialize(neighbor, infinity, infinity, keys(2)).
materialize(member, 120, infinity, keys(2)).
e1 neighbor(@X,Y) :- periodic(@X,E,0,1), env(@X,H,Y), H = "neighbor".
e2 member(@X,A,S,T,L) :- periodic(@X,E,0,1), T = f_now(), S = 0, L = 1, A = X.
e3 member(@X,Y,S,T,L) :- periodic(@X,E,0,1), neighbor(@X,Y), T = f_now(),
                          S = 0, L = 1.
e4 sequence(@X,Sequence) :- periodic(@X,E,0,1), Sequence = 0.

Figure 6.2: Narada materialized tables and initialization rules.

The materialized table `member` is a soft-state relation with lifetime of 120 s, and have unbounded size. The `neighbor` and `sequence` tables are hard-state relations. Though not explicitly specified in the `materialize` statements, the `neighbor` contains tuples of the form `neighbor(MyAddr, NeighborAddr)` and the `member` table contains tuples of the form member(MyAddr, MemberAddr, MemberS, MemberInsertionTime, MemberLive). MemberLive is a boolean indicating whether the local node believes a member is alive or has failed.

Rule `e1` initializes the neighbor table at each node based on its local env table which contains its initial set of neighbors that have been preloaded into the table when the node is started. Rules `e2-4` are used to initialize the `member` table and `sequence` tables respectively. As described in Chapter 2, `periodic(@X,E,T,K)` is a built-in event predicate that is used to generate a stream of `periodic` tuples at node X with random event identifier E every T seconds for up to K tuples. Hence, the initialization rules `e1` and `e2` are only invoked once. Rule `e2-3` initialize the `member` table at each node to itself and its initial set of neighbors. The `sequence(@X,Seq)` is a hard-state relation of size 1, which stores a single tuple that keeps track of the current sequence number Seq used in the gossip protocol.

6.2.1   MEMBERSHIP LIST MAINTENANCE

r1 refreshEvent(@X) :- periodic(@X,E,5).
r2 refreshSeq@X(X,NewS) :- refreshEvent@X(X), sequence@X(X,S), NewS = S + 1.
r3 sequence@X(X,NewS) :- refreshSeq@X(X,NewS).
r4 refreshMsg(@Y,X,NewS,Addr,AS,ALive) :- refreshSeq(@X,NewS),
                              member(@X,Addr,AS,Time,ALive),
                              neighbor(@X,Y).
r5 membersCount(@X,Addr,AS,ALive,COUNT$<$*$>$) :-
                              refreshMsg(@X,Y,YS,Addr,AS,ALive),
                              member(@X,Addr,MyS,MyTime,MyLive), X != Addr.
r6 member(@X,Addr,AS,T,ALive) :- membersCount(@X,Addr,AS,ALive,C),
                              C = 0, T = f_now().
r7 member(@X,Addr,AS,T,ALive) :- membersCount(@X,Addr,AS,ALive,C),
                              member(@X,Addr,MyS,MyT,MyLive),
                              T = f_now(), C $>$ 0, MyS $<$ AS.
r8 neighbor(@X,Y) :- refresh(@X,Y,YS,A,AS,L).

Figure 6.3: Narada membership list maintenance.

At the start, each node begins with an initial neighbor set. Narada then periodically gossips with neighbors to refresh membership information. In Figure 6.3, the rules r1-r9 specify the rules for the periodic maintenance of the membership lists.

Rule r1 generates a `requestEvent` tuple every 5 s at node X. The request interval is set by the programmer and is used to determine the rate at which nodes in the Narada exchange membership lists.

Before a Narada node can refresh its neighbors' membership lists, it must update its own sequence number, stored in the `sequence` table. Upon generating a `refreshEvent`, rule r2 creates a new refresh sequence number NewS for X by incrementing the currently stored sequence number NewS in the `sequence` table. Rule r3 updates the stored sequence number. Because `sequence` is a materialized table, whenever a new `sequence` tuple is produced, as is done with rule r3, it is implicitly inserted into the associated table. Since the primary key is the sequence number itself, this new `sequence` tuple replaces the existing tuple based on the update semantics defined in Chapter 2.

In rule r4, the `refreshSeq(@X,NewS)` that is generated is then used to generate a `refresh` message tuple that is sent to each of X's neighbors. Each `refresh` message tuple contains information about a membership entry as well as the current sequence number NewS.

Upon receiving the `refresh` message, rule r5 checks to see if the member `Addr` reported in the `refresh` message exists in the membership list. If such a member does not exist, the new member is inserted into the membership table (rule r6). If the member already exists, it is inserted into the membership table only if the sequence number in the `refresh` message is larger than that of the existing sequence number in the membership list (rule r7). The function f_now() is used to timestamp each member tuple stored.

To join the mesh, a new node need only know one member of the mesh, placing that member into its neighbor table. Rule r8 ensures that whenever a node receives a refresh message from its neighbor, it adds the sender to its neighbor set. This ensures that neighbor relationships are mutual.

6.2.2   NEIGHBOR SELECTION

There are two aspects of neighbor selection in Narada: first, evicting neighbors that are no longer responding to heartbeats (i.e., periodically generated ping messages that check whether nodes are still alive), and second, to select neighbors that meet certain user-defined criteria.

Figure 6.3 shows the rules 11–14 that can be used to check neighbor liveness. Every second, rule 11 initiates a neighbor check by which rule 12 declares *dead* a neighboring member that has failed to refresh for longer than 20 s. Dead neighbors are deleted from the neighbor table by rule 13 and rule 14 sets a dead neighbor's member entry to be "dead" and further propagated to the rest of the mesh during refreshes.

l1 neighborProbe(@X) :- periodic(@X,E,1).
l2 deadNeighbor(@X,Y) :- neighborProbe(@X), T = f_now(),
                           neighbor(@X,Y), member(@X,Y,YS,YT,L), T - YT > 20.
l3 delete neighbor(@X,Y) :- deadNeighbor(@X,Y).
l4 member(@X,Neighbor,DeadSequence,T,Live) :- deadNeighbor(@X,Neighbor),
                        member(@X,Neighbor,S,T1,L), Live = 0,
                        DeadSequence = S + 1, T = f_now().

Figure 6.4: Rules for neighbor liveness checks.

n0 pingEvent(@X,Y,E,MAX<R>) :- periodic(@X,E,2), member(@X,Y,U,V,Z),
                        R = f_rand().
n1 ping(@Y,X,E,T) :- pingEvent(@X,Y,E,MR), T = f_now().
n2 pong(@X,Y,E,T) :- ping(@Y,X,E,T).
n3 latency(@X,Y,T) :- pong@X(X,Y,E,T1), T = f_now() - T1.
n4 ugain(@X,Z,SUM<UGain>) :- latency(@X,Z,T), bestPathHop(@Z,Y,W,C),
                        bestPathHop(@X,Y,Z,UCurr), UNew = T + C,
                        UNew < UCurr, UGain = (UCurr - UNew) / UCurr.
n5 neighbor(@X,Z) :- ugain(@X,Z,UGain), UGain > addThresh.

Figure 6.5: Rules for neighbor selection based on latency.

Figure 6.5 shows the rules (n0–n3) for probing neighbors for latency measurements. Every 2 s, rule n0 picks a member at random with which to measure round-trip latency. Specifically, it associates a random number with each known member, and then chooses the member associated with the maximum random number. Recall that *aggregate<fields>* denotes an aggregation function, MAX in this example. When a pingEvent tuple is generated, rule n1 pings the randomly chosen member stored in the event, rule n2 echoes that ping, and rule n3 computes the round-trip latency of the exchange.

Nodes use such latency measurements—along with the paths computed by a routing protocol operating on top of the mesh—to compute a utility function. A node may choose a new member to add to its current neighbor set, if adding the new member increases its utility gain above an *addition threshold*. Similarly, if the cost of maintaining a current neighbor is greater than a *removal threshold*, the node may break its link with that neighbor.

Rules n4 and n5 in Figure 6.5 show how neighbor addition would work in an NDlog implementation of Narada. Each node is assumed to maintain a routing table over the mesh which contains for each member the next hop to that member and the cost of the resulting path; e.g., bestPathHop(@S,D,Z,C) indicates that node S must route via next-hop node Z to get to destination D with a path latency of C. This bestPathHop table can be computed by running the *distance-vector* protocol described in Section 5.3, taking as input the neighbor table as the input topology.

Rule n4 measures the utility gain that could be obtained if node Z were to become X's immediate neighbor, as per the Narada definition [Chu et al., 2000]. For an individual destination Y, this is computed by taking the latency of Z's path to Y and adding the latency between X and Z to it. If this new path latency (assuming Z becomes the next hop from X) is lower than the current latency of X's route to Y, then the relative decrease in latency contributes to the utility gain by adding neighbor Z. If this utility gain is above a threshold addThresh, then rule n5 adds this new neighbor.

6.3   CHORD DISTRIBUTED HASH TABLE

DN-Chord is a full-fledged implementation of the Chord distributed hash table [Stoica et al., 2001] implemented in 48 NDlog rules.

Chord is essentially a mechanism for maintaining a ring-based network and routing efficiently on it. Figure 6.6 shows an example of a Chord ring. Each node in the Chord ring has a unique 160-bit node identifier. For simplicity, the figure shows them as integers ranging from 0 to 60. Each Chord node is responsible for storing objects within a range of key-space. This is done by assigning each object with key K to the first node whose identifier is equal to or follows K in the identifier space. This node is called the *successor* of the key K. Note that data items and nodes are mapped into the same identifier space. Therefore, each node also has a successor: the node with the next-higher identifier. For example, the objects with key 42 and 56 are served by node 58.

In Chord, each node maintains the IP addresses of multiple successors to form a ring of nodes that is resilient to failure. Once a node has joined the Chord ring, it maintains network state for S successors in the ring (the succ table) with the closest identifier distance to the node, and a single predecessor (the pred table of size 1) that stores the address of the node whose identifier just

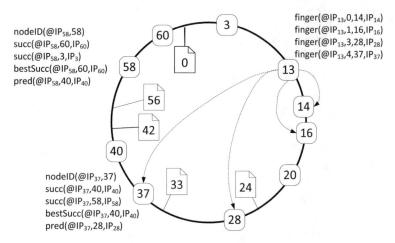

Figure 6.6: A Chord ring with the network state for node 58 and 37, the finger entries for node 13, and stored objects 0, 24, 33, 42 and 56. The dotted lines denote the fingers for node 13.

precedes the node. The bestSucc stores the address of the successor whose identifier is the closest among all the successors to the current node. For example, if $S = 2$, the successors of node 58 in Figure 6.6 are 60 and 3, its best successor is 60 and its predecessor is 40.

In order to perform scalable lookups, each Chord node also holds a finger table, pointing at peers whose identifier distances exponentially increase by powers of two from itself. The entries in the finger table are used for efficiently routing lookup requests for specific keys. There are typically 160 finger entries at each Chord node with identifier N, where the ith entry stores the node that is responsible for the key $2^i + N$. In the example Chord ring, node 13 has finger entries to nodes 14, 16, 28 and 37, as denoted by the dotted lines.

6.3.1   CHORD NETWORK STATE

Figure 6.7 shows the materialized tables that are used to store the network state of DN-Chord. For convenience, we also show the corresponding schemas of the tables with their abbreviations are shown in Figure 6.8.

Each node stores a single landmark tuple denoting the address of the node that it uses to join the Chord network (this is known as the landmark node). It also stores a nodeID tuple that contains its node identifier. In addition, each node stores the network state for Chord in the succ, pred, bestSucc and finger tables. To illustrate, Figure 6.6 shows the network state stored at node 58 that consists of the following tuples:

- A nodeID(@IP$_{58}$,58) tuple, where IP$_{58}$ denotes the IP address of node 58, and 58 is the actual identifier itself;

```
materialize(nodeID, infinity, 1, keys(1)).
materialize(landmark, infinity, 1, keys(1)).
materialize(finger, 180, 160, keys(2)).
materialize(uniqueFinger, 180, 160, keys(2)).
materialize(bestSucc, 180, 1, keys(1)).
materialize(succ, 30, 16, keys(2)).
materialize(pred, infinity, 1, keys(1)).
materialize(join, 10, 5, keys(1)).
materialize(pendingPing, 10, infinity, keys(3)).
materialize(fFix, 180, 160, keys(2)).
materialize(nextFingerFix, 180, 1, keys(1)).
```

Figure 6.7: Materialized tables for DN-Chord.

Predicate	Schema
nodeID(@NI,N)	nodeID(@NodeIP,NodeID)
landmark(@NI,N)	landmark(@NodeIP,NodeID)
finger(@NI,I,BI,B)	finger(@NodeIP,EntryNumber,BestFingerIP,BestFingerID)
uniqueFinger(@NI,I,BI,B)	uniqueFinger(@NodeIP,FingerIP)
bestSucc(@NI,N)	bestSuccessor(@NodeIP,NodeID)
succ(@NI,N)	successor(@NodeIP,NodeID)
pred(@NI,N)	predecessor(@NodeIP,NodeID)
join(@NI,E)	join(@NodeIP,EventID)
pendingPing(@NI,PI,E,T)	pendingPing(@nodeIP,PingNodeID,EventID,PingTime)
lookup(@NI,K,R,E)	lookup(@currentNodeIP,Key,RequestingNode,EventID)
lookupResults(@NI,K,R,RI,E)	lookupResults(@RequestingNodeIP,Key,ResultKey, ResultNodeIP,EventID)

Figure 6.8: Predicates and corresponding schemas of materialized tables and lookup events used in DN-Chord.

- $succ(@IP_{58},60,IP_{60})$ and $succ(@IP_{58},3,IP_3)$ tuples storing the immediate identifier and IP addresses of the two successors of node 58; and

- $bestSucc(@IP_{58},60,IP_{60})$ and $pred(@IP_{58},40,IP_{40})$ tuples storing the identifier and IP addresses of the best successor and predecessor of node 58.

The figure also shows similar network state for node 37, and the four finger entries for node 13: $finger(@IP_{13},0,14,IP_{14})$, $finger(@IP_{13},1,16,IP_{16})$, $finger(@IP_{13},3,28,IP_{28})$ and $finger(@IP_{13},4,37,IP_{37})$. Since there can be multiple finger entries pointing to the same node, the `uniqueFinger` table is used to keep track of only the unique nodes that are pointed by the finger entries.

In addition, there are other materialized tables such as `join`, `pendingPing`, `fFix` and `nextFingerFix` that are used to store intermediate state in the DN-Chord implementation. The rest of the section demonstrates how different aspects of Chord can be specified in NDlog: *joining the Chord network*, *ring maintenance*, *finger maintenance and routing*, and *failure detection*.

6.3.2   JOINING THE CHORD NETWORK

i1 pred(@NI,P,PI) :- periodic(@NI,E,0,1), P = "NIL", PI = "NIL".
i2 nextFingerFix(@NI, 0) :- periodic(@NI,E,0,1).
i3 landmark(@NI,LI) :- periodic(@NI,E,0,1), env(@NI,H,LI), H = "landmark".
i4 nodeID(@NI,N) :- periodic(@NI,E,0,1), env(@NI,H,N), H = "nodeID".

Figure 6.9: Rules for initializing a Chord node.

When a node is started, rules i1–i4 from Figure 6.9 can immediately deduce facts that set the initial state of the node. Rule i1 sets the `pred` to point to NIL indicating that there are no predecessors. Rule i2 initializes the `nextFingerFix` to be 0 for use in finger maintenance, as described in Section 6.3.4. Rule i3 initializes a `landmark(@NI,LI)` tuple in the `landmark` table of each node NI storing the address of the landmark node LI. This address is input to the DN system via a preloaded local `env` table. The landmark LI is set to NIL if the node itself is the landmark. Each node also stores a `nodeID(@NI,N)` tuple that contains the random node identifier N that is also preloaded from the local `env` table (Rule i4).

j1 joinEvent(@NI,E) :- periodic(@NI,E,1,2).
j2 join(@NI,E) :- joinEvent(@NI,E).
j3 joinReq(@LI,N,NI,E) :- joinEvent(@NI,E), nodeID(@NI,N),
                          landmark(@NI,LI), LI != "NIL".
j4 succ(@NI,N,NI) :- landmark(@NI,LI), joinEvent(@NI,E),
                     nodeID(@NI,N), LI = "NIL".
j5 lookup(@LI,N,NI,E) :- joinReq(@LI,N,NI,E).
j6 succ(@NI,S,SI) :- join(@NI,E), lookupResults(@NI,K,S,SI,E).

Figure 6.10: Rules for joining the Chord ring.

Figure 6.10 shows the rules for joining the Chord ring. To enter the ring, a node NI generates a `joinEvent` tuple locally (rule j1) whose arrival triggers rules j2-j6. Rule j2 creates a `join` tuple upon the arrival of the `joinEvent` tuple. In rule j3, if the landmark node is known (i.e., not NIL), a `joinReq` tuple is sent to the landmark node; otherwise rule j4 sets the node to point to itself as a successor, forming an overlay by itself and awaiting others to join in. When the landmark receives a `joinReq` tuple, rule j5 initiates a lookup from the landmark node for the successor of the joining node's identifier N, and set the return address of the lookup to be NI. If the lookup is successful, a `lookupResults` event is received at node NI. Rule j6 then defines the joining node's successor (`succ` table) to be the result of the lookup.

6.3.3   CHORD RING MAINTENANCE

sb1 succ(@NI,P,PI) :- periodic(@NI,E,10), nodeID(@NI,N),
                      bestSucc(@NI,S,SI), pred(@SI,P,PI),
                      PI != "NIL", P in (N,S).
sb2 succ(@NI,S1,SI1) :- periodic(@NI,E,10), succ(@NI,S,SI), succ(@SI,S1,SI1).
sb3 pred(@SI,N,NI) :- periodic(@NI,E,10), nodeID(@NI,N),
                      succ(@NI,S,SI), pred(@SI,P,PI), nodeID(@SI,N'),
                      ((PI = "NIL") || (N in (P,N'))) && (NI != SI).

Figure 6.11: Rules for ring stabilization.

After joining the Chord network, each node performs the ring maintenance protocol in order to maintain a set of successors and a single predecessor. Candidate successors (and the single predecessor) are found during the *stabilization* phase of the Chord overlay maintenance. The rules specifying the stabilization phase in Figure 6.11. Stabilization is done periodically at time intervals of 15 s by the rules sb1, sb2 and sb3. Rule sb1 ensures that a node's best successor's predecessor is also stored in its successor table. In rule sb2, each successor periodically asks all of its successors to send it their own successors. In rule sb3, a node periodically notifies its successors about itself, allowing its successors to point their respective predecessors to the notifying node if it is closer in key-space compared to their current predecessors.

n1 newSuccEvent(@NI) :- succ(@NI,S,SI).
n2 newSuccEvent(@NI) :- deleteSucc(@NI,S,SI).
n3 bestSuccDist(@NI,MIN<D>) :- newSuccEvent(@NI), nodeID(@NI,N),
                               succ(@NI,S,SI), D = S - N - 1.
n4 bestSucc(@NI,S,SI) :- succ(@NI,S,SI), bestSuccDist(@NI,D), nodeID(@NI,N),
                         D = S - N - 1.
n5 finger(@NI,0,S,SI) :- bestSucc(@NI,S,SI).

Figure 6.12: Rules for computing best successor and first finger entry.

Based on the set of candidate successors obtained from stabilization, additional rules are required in order to select the best successor, and also evict successors that are no longer required. In Figure 6.12, rule n1 generates a `newSuccEvent` event tuple upon the insertion (refresh) of a new (existing) successor. Rule n2 generates a `newSuccEvent` for deletions of an existing successor.

The newSuccEvent event tuple triggers rules n3 and n4, which are used to define as "best" the successor among those stored in the succ stored table whose identifier distance from the current node's identifier is the lowest. Rule n5 further ensures that the first finger entry (used for routing lookups) is always the same as the best successor.

---

s1 succCount(@NI,COUNT<*>) :- newSuccEvent(@NI), succ(@NI,S,SI).
s2 evictSucc(@NI) :- succCount(@NI,C), C > 4.
s3 maxSuccDist(@NI,MAX<D>) :- nodeID(@NI,N), succ(@NI,S,SI),
                    evictSucc(@NI), D = S - N - 1.
s4 delete succ(@NI,S,SI) :- nodeID(@NI,N), succ(@NI,S,SI),
                    maxSuccDist(@NI,D), D = S - N - 1.

Figure 6.13: Rules for successor selection.

As new successors are discovered, successor selection only keeps those successors closest to a node in the table, evicting at each discovery the single remaining node (rules s1–s4 in Figure 6.13).

6.3.4   FINGER MAINTENANCE AND ROUTING

---

l1 lookupResults(@R,K,S,SI,E) :- nodeID(@NI,N), lookup(@NI,K,R,E),
                    bestSucc(@NI,S,SI), K in (N,S].
l2 bestLookupDist(@NI,K,R,E,MIN<D>) :- nodeID(@NI,N),
                    lookup(@NI,K,R,E), finger(@NI,I,B,BI),
                    D = K - B - 1, B in (N,K).
l3 lookup(MIN<@BI>,K,R,E) :- nodeID(@NI,N),
                    bestLookupDist(@NI,K,R,E,D), finger(@NI,I,B,BI),
                    D = K - B - 1, B in (N,K).

Figure 6.14: Rules for recursive lookups in Chord.

The finger table is used in Chord to route lookup requests. Figure 6.14 shows the three rules that are used to implement lookups in Chord. Each lookup(@NI,K,R,E) event tuple denotes a lookup request at node NI for key K, originates from node R with event identifier E.

From the earlier introduction to the Chord protocol, all lookup requests for key K seek the node whose identifier is the immediate successor on the ring of K. Rule l1 is the base case, returning a successful lookup result if the received lookup seeks a key K found between the receiving node's identifier and that of its best successor. Rule l2 is used in non-base cases, to find the minimum distance (in key identifier space modulo 2^{160}) from the local node's fingers to K for every finger node BI whose identifier B lies between the local node's identifier N and K. Rule l3 then selects one of the finger entries with the minimum distance to key K as the target node BI to receive the lookup request. Since there can be multiple such finger entries, the min<BI> aggregate ensures that only one of the finger entries receives the forwarded lookup.

---

f1 fFix(@NI,E,I) :- periodic(@NI,E,10), nextFingerFix(@NI,I).
f2 fFixEvent(@NI,E,I) :- fFix(@NI,E,I).
f3 lookup(@NI,K,NI,E) :- fFixEvent(@NI,E,I), nodeID(@NI,N), K = 0x1I << I + N.
f4 eagerFinger(@NI,I,B,BI) :- fFix(@NI,E,I), lookupResults(@NI,K,B,BI,E).
f5 finger(@NI,I,B,BI) :- eagerFinger(@NI,I,B,BI).
f6 eagerFinger(@NI,I,B,BI) :- eagerFinger(@NI,I1,B,BI),
                  nodeID(@NI,N), I = I1 + 1,
                  K = 0x1I << I + N, K in (N,B), NI != BI.
f7 delete fFix(@NI,E,I1) :- eagerFinger(@NI,I,B,BI), fFix(@NI,E,I1),
                  I > 0, I1 = I - 1.
f8 nextFingerFix(@NI,0) :- eagerFinger(@NI,I,B,BI), ((I = 159) || (BI = NI)).
f9 nextFingerFix(@NI,I) :- eagerFinger(@NI,I1,B,BI),
                  nodeID(@NI,N), I = I1 + 1,
                  K = 0x1I << I + N, K in (B,N), NI != BI.
f10 uniqueFinger(@NI,BI) :- finger(@NI,I,B,BI).

Figure 6.15: Rules for generating finger entries.

Figure 6.15 shows the rules for generating the entries in the finger table. There are two additional materialized tables fFix and nextFingerFix that store intermediate state for the finger fixing protocol. The nextFingerFix table stores one tuple nextFingerFix(@NI,I) that stores the next finger entry I to be picked for fixing at node NI.

Every 10 s, rule f1 selects the I finger to fix, and then generates a fFix(@NI,E,I) tuple that denotes that the I finger is selected for fixing with event identifier E. This results in the generating of a fFixEvent(@NI,E,I) event tuple in rule f2 which will generate a lookup request for key $K = 2^I + N$ with the corresponding event identifier E. When the lookup succeeds, rule f4 receives a lookupResults event tuple, which it then uses to update all the corresponding finger entries (f5-6). Rules f7-f9 then deletes the fFix tuple, and then increments the I field of nextFingerFix by 1 for fixing the next finger entry in the next period. Rule f10 sets the uniqueFinger based on new finger entries.

6.3.5   FAILURE DETECTION

Figure 6.16 shows the rules that a node utilizes for sending keep-alive messages to its neighbors. The rules are similar to that of the *Ping-Pong* program presented in Chapter 2. At regular intervals of 5 s, each node generates one pendingPing tuple for each one of its neighbors (rules pp1, pp2 and pp3). This results in pingReq messages that are periodically (every 3 s as indicated in rule pp3)

pp1 pendingPing(@NI,SI,E1,T) :- periodic(@NI,E,5), succ(@NI,S,SI),
                     E1 = f_rand(), SI != NI, T = f_now().
pp2 pendingPing(@NI,PI,E1,T) :- periodic(@NI,E,5), pred(@NI,P,PI),
                     E1 = f_rand(), PI ! = "NIL", T = f_now().
pp3 pendingPing(@NI,FI,E1,T) :- periodic(@NI,E,5), uniqueFinger(@NI,FI),
                     E1 = f_rand(), T = f_now().
pp4 pingResp(@RI,NI,E) :- pingReq(@NI,RI,E).
pp5 pingReq(@PI,NI,E) :- periodic(@NI,E1,3),
                     pendingPing(@NI,PI,E,T).
pp6 delete pendingPing(@NI,SI,E,T) :- pingResp(@NI,SI,E), pendingPing(@NI,SI,E,T).

Figure 6.16: Rules for sending keep-alives.

fd1 nodeFailure(@NI,PI,E1,D) :- periodic(@NI,E,1), pendingPing(@NI,PI,E1,T),
                     T1 = f_now(), D = T-T1, D > 7.
fd2 delete pendingPing(@NI,PI,E,T) :- nodeFailure(@NI,PI,E,D),
                     pendingPing(@NI,PI,E,T).
fd3 deleteSucc(@NI,S,SI) :- succ(@NI,S,SI), nodeFailure(@NI,SI,E,D).
fd4 delete succ(@NI,S,SI) :- deleteSucc(@NI,S,SI).
fd5 pred(@NI,"NIL","NIL") :- pred(@NI,P,PI), nodeFailure(@NI,PI,E,D).
fd6 delete finger(@NI,I,B,BI) :- finger(@NI,I,B,BI), nodeFailure(@NI,BI,E,D).
fd7 delete uniqueFinger(@NI,FI) :- uniqueFinger(@NI,FI), nodeFailure(@NI,FI,E,D).

Figure 6.17: Rules for failure detection of successors, predecessors and fingers.

sent to the respective neighbors for the lifetime of each pendingPing tuple. These pendingPings are deleted upon receiving the corresponding pingResp messages.

Figure 6.17 shows the rules for detecting failure of successors, predecessors and fingers. Here, rule fd1 generates nodeFailure events when there are outstanding pendingPing tuples that are unanswered after a period of time. The choices of 7 s in rule fd1 and 3 s in rule pp5 determine the frequency in which pingReq messages are sent, and the number unanswered replies that are required before concluding that a node is "dead." In this example, a node is considered "dead" if there are two successive unanswered pingReq messages. The nodeFailure event then results in deletion of pendingPing, succ and finger entries, and resetting the single pred entry (rules fd3-fd7). A deleteSucc event is generated to allow the recomputation of the best successor in rules n2-n5.

6.3.6   SUMMARY OF CHORD

Chord is specified in only 48 rules, which is two orders of magnitude less code compared to an equivalent C++ implementation [MIT Chord]. In addition, in order to deal with issues related to message delivery, acknowledgments, failure detection and timeouts, there is extensive use of soft-state tables and soft-state rules presented in Chapter 2.

As a summary, in addition to the `materialize` statements and initialization rules `i1-i4`, the NDlog rules for Chord can be categorized into three functionalities of a typical overlay network that we presented earlier.

- **Overlay formation and maintenance:** Rules `j1-j6` are used by a node joining the Chord network via a landmark. Once a node has joined the ring, rules `sb1-sb3` are used to execute the ring stabilization to learn about new successors and refine the predecessor. Based on the successors learned, rules `n1-n5` are used for selecting the best successor, and rules `s1-s4` are used for evicting unnecessary successors. To ensure that all overlay neighbors are alive, rules `pp1-pp6` and `fd1-fd7` for periodically pinging all successors, predecessors and finger entries, and deleting them if they do not respond to heartbeats.

- **Routing:** Given the basic ring network, rules `f1-f10` for generating finger table entries that ensures scalable lookups.

- **Forwarding:** With the finger table in place, rules `l1-l3` are used for routing lookup requests via the finger table.

Overlay formation constitutes the majority of Chord rules, and clearly illustrates the additional challenges in specifying declarative overlays compared to the relatively simpler NDlog programs for implementing routing protocols presented in Chapter 5.

6.4   EVALUATION

This section presents performance results of the Narada mesh and the DN-Chord DHT. The experiments are carried out using P2 [P2], on 100 machines on the Emulab testbed [Emulab]. In both overlay networks, the latency between any two overlay nodes is set to 100 ms, and link capacity is set to 10 MBps.

6.4.1   NARADA MESH FORMATION

The first experiment evaluates the Narada specifications on mesh formation. The experiment consists of 100 Narada nodes, one on each Emulab node. All nodes join the network over a span of 10 s. Each Narada node has an initial set of neighbors, and at regular intervals of 5 s, propagate its entire membership list to its neighbors. The measurement metrics include the per-node bandwidth (KBps) of periodically sending the membership list in the steady state, and also the convergence time (seconds) taken for all Narada nodes have achieved full membership knowledge of the entire network.

Figure 6.18 shows the CDF of membership at each node as a fraction of the entire network size over time (seconds) for a network size of 100 for two experimental runs (*NS=2, NS=4*) where

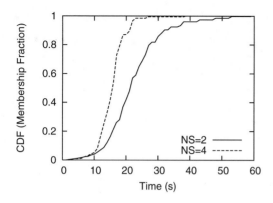

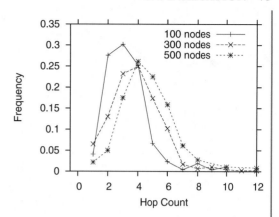

Figure 6.18: CDF of average Narada membership at each node as fraction of total network size over time (s).

Figure 6.19: Hop-count distribution for lookups.

the number of neighbors that each node has is varied (2 and 4 neighbors). Each data point (x, y) shows the average fraction y of the network that each node knows at time x. Upon convergence, all nodes learn about every other node in the network (i.e., $y = 1$).

The figure show that the Narada implementation converges on the sparser network ($NS = 2$) within 60 s, while requiring less than 40 s to converge on the denser network ($NS = 4$). The convergence time includes the initial 10 s as nodes join the Narada network. These evaluation results demonstrate the tradeoffs between bandwidth and convergence in propagating the membership list – the faster convergence of the denser network comes at the expense of bandwidth utilization ($33K\,Bps$) as compared to $13K\,Bps$ for the sparser network.

6.4.2   CHORD DHT

The next set of experiments focuses on measuring the specification for the Chord Distributed Hash Table. Chord serves as a good stress test of the declarative overlays, being relatively complex compared to other overlay examples like gossip and end-system multicast. Chord also has the advantage of being well-studied. The Chord deployment on the Emulab testbed [Emulab] consists of 100 machines (64-bit Xeon 3000 series with 2 GB memory) executing up to 500 Chord instances (5 Chord processes running on each Emulab machine). The same network topology as the Narada experiment is utilized.

Static Network Validation

The first round of experiments is to validate the high-level characteristics of the Chord overlay, using a uniform workload of DHT "lookup" requests to a static set of nodes in the overlay, with no nodes joining or leaving. This is somewhat unrealistic but it allows to validate the static properties

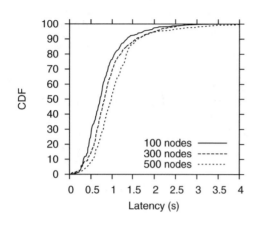

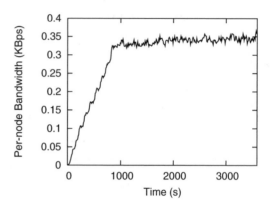

Figure 6.20: CDF for lookup latency.

Figure 6.21: Per-node bandwidth (KBps) over time (s).

of Chord. Each experiment starts with a landmark node, and all other nodes join the landmark node at regular intervals. Once all the nodes have joined the Chord overlay, lookups are issued every 15 s simultaneously (with the same lookup key K) from 10 nodes.

All lookup requests return successfully with the lookup requests. In addition, all lookups achieve 100% consistency, where all lookup requests for the same key issued from different nodes return identical results. Figures 6.19, 6.20, and 6.21 report the quantitative performance results.

Figure 6.19 shows the hop count distribution for the workload. Except for a few outliers, 99% of all lookups complete within 10 hops. The average hop count of lookups are 3.3, 4.0 and 4.5 for node sizes of 100, 300 and 500 respectively, approximating the theoretical average of $0.5 \times log_2(N)$, where N is the number of nodes.

Figure 6.20 shows the CDF of lookup latencies for different network sizes. As expected, the average latency increases in proportion to the average lookup hop count for each network size. On a 500 node static network, 99% of all lookups complete in less than 3.4 s. The average (median) latencies are 0.81 s (0.72 s), 0.92 s (0.82 s) and 1.09 s (0.98 s) for node sizes of 100, 300 and 500, respectively. The average and median latency numbers are within the same order of magnitude as the published numbers [Stoica et al., 2001] of the MIT Chord deployment.

Figure 6.21 shows the per-node bandwidth (KBps) consumption over time (in seconds) for a static DN-Chord network where fingers are fixed every 10 s, and ring stabilization (exchange of successors and predecessors among neighbors) happen every 10 s. Each node periodically sends ping messages to neighbors every 3 s. After an initial linear increase in bandwidth as nodes join the Chord ring, the bandwidth utilization stabilizes at 0.34 KBps, well within the published bandwidth consumption of 1 KBps [Rhea et al., 2004] of other high consistency and low latency DHTs.

Churn Performance

The second round of experiments focuses on the performance of the Chord implementation under varying degrees of membership churn. Again, the goal is to validate that the compact declarative specification of Chord faithfully captures its salient properties following the methodology in the Bamboo system [Rhea et al., 2004]. The experiment is performed on a 100 node Chord network. Once the network is stable, churn is induced for 20 min as follows. Periodically, a randomly selected node fails. Upon each node failure, a new node immediately joins the Chord network with a different node identifier. The interval between every node failure/restart event varies to achieve different average node session times (8, 16, 47 and 90 min).

In the steady state under constant churn, lookups for the same key are issued simultaneously from 10 different nodes every 15 s. Following the methodology in Bamboo [Rhea et al., 2004], a *consistent* lookup is defined as when a majority of the lookups (>5) see a consistent result that points to the same node that owns the key. For each group of 10 lookups, the maximum fraction of lookups that share a consistent result is computed.

Chord's churn parameters are set as follows: (1) the fix finger and ring-stabilization periods are both set to 10 s as before; (2) each node periodically send ping messages to neighbor nodes every 3 s, and remove entries from the local neighbor tables if they do not respond to two successive pings.

Figure 6.22 shows the CDF (log-scale for Y-axis) for the *consistent fraction* of lookups, which is defined as the fraction of lookups with consistent result for each group of simultaneous lookups. To interpret the graph, each data-point (x, y) shows the fraction y of lookups with lookup consistency less than x. The results show that DN-Chord does well under low churn (session times of 90 min and 47 min), generating 99% and 96% consistent lookups. Under high churn (session times of 16 min and 8 min), it also performs well, producing 95% and 79% consistent lookups.

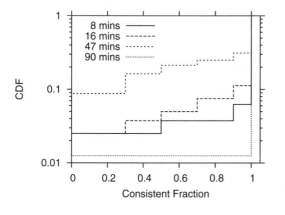

Figure 6.22: CDF for lookup consistency fraction under churn.

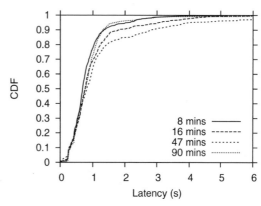

Figure 6.23: CDF for lookup latency under churn.

Figure 6.23 shows the CDF of the lookup latencies for different churn rates. At low churn rates, the lookup latencies are similar to those measured under a stable Chord network with no churn. At high churn rates, the average lookup latency increased from 0.81 s to 1.01 s and 1.32 s, respectively.

While DN-Chord performs acceptably, it clearly does not attain the published figures for the MIT implementation (at least 99.9% consistency for a session time of 47 min). Ultimately, the system evaluation rests on an assessment of the ideal tradeoff between code size and performance. It may be the case that churn performance can be at the expense of additional rules that implements lookup retries on a per-hop basis, and better failure detection techniques with adaptive timers.

6.5   SUMMARY

This chapter demonstrates the use of NDlog for expressing two complex overlay networks, namely the Narada mesh formation and a full-fledged implementation of the Chord distributed hash table in 16 and 48 rules, respectively.

The DN-Chord implementation is roughly two orders of magnitude less code than the original C++ implementation. This is a quantitative difference that is sufficiently large that it becomes qualitative: declarative programs that are a few dozen lines of code are markedly easier to understand, debug and extend than multi-thousand-line imperative programs.

CHAPTER 7

Optimization of NDlog Programs

One of the promises of a declarative approach to networking is that it can enable automatic optimizations of protocols, much as relational databases can automatically optimize queries. This not only reduces the burden on programmers, it also enables what Codd called *data independence* [Codd, 1970]: the ability for the implementation of a program to adapt to different underlying execution substrates.

The main goals in this chapter are to demonstrate that the declarative approach is amenable to automatic query optimization, and to illustrate the close connection between network optimization and query optimization. In doing so, this opens up what appears to be a rich new set of research opportunities.

The chapter is organized as follows. Section 7.1 explores the application of traditional Datalog optimizations in the declarative networking context. New techniques for multi-query optimizations and cost-based optimizations are proposed in Sections 7.2 and 7.3, respectively. To validate our proposed optimizations, Section 7.4 presents a performance evaluation of the DN engine executing optimized declarative routing queries on the Emulab testbed.

7.1   TRADITIONAL DATALOG OPTIMIZATIONS

Declarative networking applies three traditional Datalog optimization techniques: *aggregate selections*, *magic sets* and *predicate reordering*. The primary focus of optimizations is on declarative routing queries, which are variants of transitive closure queries.

7.1.1   AGGREGATE SELECTIONS

A naïve execution of the *Shortest-path* program computes all possible paths, even those paths that do not contribute to the eventual shortest paths. This inefficiency can be avoided with an optimization technique known as *aggregate selections* [Furfaro et al., 2002, Sudarshan and Ramakrishnan, 1991].

Aggregate selections are useful when the running state of a monotonic aggregate function can be used to prune program evaluation. For example, by applying aggregate selections to the *Shortest-path* program, each node only needs to propagate the current shortest paths for each destination to neighbors. This propagation can be done whenever a shorter path is derived.

A potential problem with this approach is that the propagation of new shortest paths may be unnecessarily aggressive, resulting in wasted communication. As an enhancement, a modified scheme called *periodic aggregate selections*, works by getting each node to buffer up new paths received from neighbors, recomputes any new shortest paths incrementally, and then propagates the new shortest paths periodically. The periodic technique has the potential for reducing network bandwidth consumption, at the expense of increasing convergence time. It is useful for queries whose input tuples tend to arrive over the network in an order that is not positively correlated with the monotonic aggregate, e.g., computing "shortest" paths for metrics that are not correlated with the network delays that dictate the arrival of the tuples during execution.

In addition, aggregate selections are necessary for the termination of some queries. For example, with aggregate selections, even if paths with cycles are permitted, the *Shortest-Path* program will terminate, avoiding cyclic paths of increasing lengths.

7.1.2   MAGIC SETS AND PREDICATE REORDERING

The *Shortest-Path* program computes *all-pairs* shortest paths. This leads to unnecessary overhead when querying for paths between a limited set of sources and/or destinations. This problem can be alleviated by applying two optimization techniques: *magic-sets rewriting* and *predicate reordering*.

Magic-Sets Rewriting: A query rewrite technique called *magic sets rewriting* [Bancilhon et al., 1986, Beeri and Ramakrishnan, 1987] can be used to limit computation to the relevant portion of the network. The Magic Sets method is closely related to methods such as Alexander [Rohmer et al., 1986] and QSQ [Vieille, 1986], all of which are designed to avoid computing facts that do not contribute to the final answer to a recursive query. The proposed processing techniques in Chapter 4 are based on bottom-up (or forward-chaining) evaluation [Ramakrishnan and Sudarshan, 1999] where the bodies of the rules are evaluated to derive the heads. This has the advantage of permitting set-oriented optimizations while avoiding infinite recursive loops, but may result in computing redundant facts not required by the program. For example, even when the *Shortest-Path* program (Figure 2.5 in Chapter 2) specifies shortestPath(@a,b,Z,P,C) as the "goal" of the query, naïvely applying bottom-up evaluation results in the computation of *all* paths between *all* pairs of nodes.

The magic sets rewrite avoids these redundant computations and yet retains the two advantages of bottom-up evaluation. The key ideas behind the rewrite include: (1) the introduction of "magic predicates" to represent variable bindings in queries that a top-down search would ask; and (2) the use of "supplementary predicates" to represent how answers are passed from left-to-right in a rule. The rewritten program is still evaluated in a bottom-up fashion, but the additional predicates generated during the rewrite ensure that there are no redundant computations.

The use of magic sets is illustrated in an example: by modifying rule sp1 from the *Shortest-Path* program, the following program in Figure 7.1 computes only those paths leading to destinations in the magicDst table.

Rule sp1-d initializes 1-hop paths for destinations whose magicDst(@D) is present in the magicDst table. Rule m1 adds a magicDst(@a) fact in the magicDst table. Intuitively, the set of

```
#include(sp2,sp3,sp4)
sp1-d path(@S,D,D,P,C) :- magicDst(@D),link(@S,D,C), P = f_init(S,D).
m1 magicDst(@a).
Query shortestPath(@S,a,P,C).
```

Figure 7.1: Shortest-Path program with magic sets.

`magicDst(@D)` facts is used as a "magic predicate" or "filter" in the rules defining paths. This ensures that rule `sp2` propagates paths to selected destinations based on the `magicDst` table (in this case, paths to only node a). The shortest paths are then computed as before using rules `sp3` and `sp4`.

Predicate Reordering: The use of magic sets in the previous program is not useful for pruning paths from sources. This is because paths are derived in a *"Bottom-Up" (BU)* fashion starting from destination nodes, where the derived paths are shipped "backwards" along neighbor links from destinations to sources. Interestingly, switching the search strategy can be done simply by *reordering* the `path` and link predicates. Recall from Chapter 2 that predicates in a rule are evaluated in a default left-to-right order. This has the effect of turning sp2 from a *right-recursive* to a *left-recursive* rule: the recursive predicate is now to the left of the non-recursive predicate in the rule body. Together with the use of magic sets, the *Magic-Shortest-Path* program in Figure 7.2 allows filtering on *both* sources and *destinations*.

```
sp1-sd pathDst(S,@D,D,P,C) :- magicSrc(@S), link(@S,D,C),
                              P = f_init(S,D).
sp2-sd pathDst(S,@D,Z,P,C) :- pathDst(S,@Z,Z1,P1,C1),link(@Z,D,C2),
                              C = C1 + C2, P = f_concatPath(P1,D).
sp3-sd spCost(@D,S,MIN<C>) :- magicDst(@D),pathDst(S,@D,Z,P,C).
sp4-sd shortestPath(S,@D,P,C) :- spCost(S,@D,C),pathDst(S,@D,Z,P,C).
```

Figure 7.2: Magic-Shortest-Path program.

The left-recursive *Shortest-Path* program computes 1-hop paths starting from each `magicSrc` using rule `sp1-sd`. Rule `sp2-sd` then recursively computes new paths by following all reachable links, and stores these paths as `pathDst` tuples at each destination. Rules `sp3-sd` and `sp4-sd` then filter relevant paths based on `magicDst`, and compute the shortest paths, which can then be propagated along the shortest paths back to the source node. In fact, executing the program in this *"Top-Down" (TD)* fashion resembles a network protocol called *dynamic source routing* (DSR) [Johnson and Maltz, 1996] presented in Section 5.3.4 as a declarative routing example program. DSR is proposed for ad-hoc wireless environments, where the high rate of change in the network makes such targeted path discovery more efficient compared to computing all-pairs shortest paths.

Interestingly, the use of magic sets and predicate reordering reveals close connections between query optimizations and network optimizations. By specifying routing protocols in NDlog at a high level, the two well-known protocols—one for wired networks and one for wireless—differ only in applying a standard query optimization: the order of two predicates in a single rule body. In addition, the use of magic sets allows us to do a more targeted path discovery suited in the wireless setting. Ultimately, such connections between query optimizations and network optimizations will provide a better understanding of the design space of routing protocols.

7.2 MULTI-QUERY OPTIMIZATIONS

In a distributed setting, it is likely that many related queries will be concurrently executed independently by different nodes. A key requirement for scalability is the ability to share common query computations (e.g., pairwise shortest paths) among a potentially large number of queries. Two basic strategies for multi-query sharing in this environment are used: *query-result caching* and *opportunistic message sharing*.

Query-Result Caching. Consider the *Magic-Shortest-Path* program where node a computes shortestPath(@a,d,[a,b,d],6) to node d. This cached value can be reused by all queries for destination d that pass through a, e.g., the path from e to d. Currently, our implementation generates the cache internally, building a cache of all the query results (in this case shortestPath tuples) as they are sent back on the reverse path to the source node. Since the subpaths of shortest paths are optimal, these can also be cached as an enhancement.

Opportunistic Message Sharing. In the previous example, different nodes (src/dst) could share their work in running the *same* program logic with different constants. Sharing across *different* queries is a more difficult problem, since it is non-trivial to detect query containment in general [Calvanese et al., 2003]. However, in many cases, there can be correlation in the message patterns even for different queries. One example arises when different queries request "shortest" paths based on different metrics, such as latency, reliability and bandwidth; path tuples being propagated for these separate queries may be identical modulo the metric attribute being optimized.

In *opportunistic message sharing*, multiple outgoing tuples that share common attribute values are essentially joined into one tuple if they are outbound to the same destination; they are re-partitioned at the receiving end. In order to improve the odds of achieving this sharing, outbound tuples may be buffered for a time and combined in batch before being sent.

As an alternative to this opportunistic sharing at the network level, one can achieve explicit sharing at a logical level, e.g., using correlated aggregate selections for pruning different paths based on a combination of metrics. For example, consider running two queries: one that computes shortest latency paths, and another that computes max-bandwidth paths. These programs can be rewritten into a single NDlog program that checks two aggregate selections, i.e., only prune paths that satisfy *both* aggregate selections.

7.3   HYBRID REWRITES

Currently, rules are expressed using a left-recursive (BU) or right-recursive (TD) syntax (Section 7.1.2). The main goal during query execution is *network efficiency* (i.e., reducing the burden on the underlying network), which, typically, also implies faster query convergence. It is not difficult to see that neither BU nor TD execution is universally superior under different network/query settings. Even in the simple case of a shortest-path discovery query shortestPath(@S,@D,P,C) between two given nodes (@S,@D), minimizing message overhead implies that the query processor should prefer a strategy that restricts execution to "sparser" regions of the network (e.g., doing a TD exploration from a sparsely-connected source @S).

Cost-based query optimization techniques are needed to guarantee effective query execution plans. While such techniques have long been studied in the context of relational database systems, optimizing distributed recursive queries for network efficiency raises several novel challenges. The remainder of this section briefly discusses proposed ideas in this area and their ties with work in network protocols.

The Neighborhood Function Statistic. As with traditional query optimization, cost-based techniques must rely on appropriate *statistics* for the underlying execution environment that can drive the optimizer's choices. One such key statistic for network efficiency is the *local neighborhood density* $N()$. Formally, $N(X, r)$ is the number of distinct network nodes within r hops of node X. The neighborhood function is a natural generalization of the size of the transitive closure (i.e., reachability set) of a node, that can be estimated locally (e.g., through other recursive queries running in the background/periodically). $N(X, r)$ can also be efficiently *approximated* through approximate-counting techniques using small (log-size) messages [Palmer et al., 2002]. To see the relevance of $N()$ for the query-optimization problem, consider the example shortestPath(@s,@d,P,C) query, and let dist(s, d) denote the distance of s, d in the network. A TD search would explore the network starting from node s, and (modulo network batching) result in a total of $N(s, \text{dist}(s, d))$ messages (since it reaches all nodes within a radius of dist(s, d) from s). Note that each node only forwards the query message once, even though it may receive it along multiple paths. Similarly, the cost for a BU query execution is $N(d, \text{dist}(s, d))$. However, neither of these strategies is necessarily optimal in terms of message cost. The optimal strategy is actually a *hybrid scheme* that "splits" the search radius dist(s, d) between s and d to minimize the overall messages; that is, it first finds r_s and r_d such that:

$$(r_s, r_d) = \arg \min_{r_s + r_d = \text{dist}(s,d)} \{ N(s, r_s) + N(d, r_d) \},$$

and then runs concurrent TD and BU searches from nodes s and d (with radii r_s and r_d, respectively). At the end of this process, both the TD and the BU search have intersected in at least one network node, which can easily assemble the shortest (s, d) path. While the above optimization problem is trivially solvable in $O(\text{dist}(s, d))$ time, generalizing this hybrid-rewrite scheme to the case of multiple sources and destinations raises difficult algorithmic challenges. And, of course, adapting such cost-based optimization algorithms to work in the distributed, dynamic setting poses system challenges. Finally, note that neighborhood-function information can also provide a valuable indicator for the utility of a node as a result cache (Section 7.2) during query processing.

Adaptive Network Routing Protocols. As further illustrations on the close connection between networking routing and query optimizations, the networking literature has considered adaptive routing protocols that strongly resemble the use of hybrid rewrites; hence, this is an important area for future investigation and generalization. One interesting example is the class of *Zone-Routing Protocols* (ZRP) [Haas, 1997]. A ZRP algorithm works by each node precomputing *k-hop-radius* shortest paths to neighboring nodes (in its "zone") using a BU strategy. Then, a shortest-path route from a source to destination is computed in a TD fashion, using essentially the *Magic-Shortest-Path* program described above, utilizing any precomputed shortest paths along the way. Each node sets its zone radius k adaptively based on the density and rate of change of links in its neighborhood; in fact, recent work [Ramasubramanian et al., 2003] on adjusting the zone radius for ZRP-like routing uses exactly the neighborhood-function statistic.

7.4   EVALUATION OF OPTIMIZATIONS

This section examines the effectiveness of the optimizations that are proposed in this chapter. The workload is primarily based on declarative routing protocols executed using P2 [P2], and measure four variants of the same *Shortest-Path* program, differing in the link metric each seeks to minimize. Our experimental setup is similar to Section 5.6, where the *Shortest-Path* program is executed on an overlay network in which each node has four neighbors. In addition, for each neighbor link, we generate additional metrics that include reliability, and a randomly generated value. Note that the reliability metric for each link is synthetically generated to be correlated with latency.

On all the graphs, these queries are labeled by their link metric: *Hop-Count, Latency, Reliability* and *Random*, respectively. Recall from Section 5.6.2 that *Random* serves as the stress case: it is expected to have the worst performance among the different metrics. This is due to aggregate selections being less effective when the aggregate metric is uncorrelated with the network latency.

7.4.1   AGGREGATE SELECTIONS

In order to investigate the effectiveness of aggregate selections for different queries, Figure 7.3 shows the per-node bandwidth usage against time for the *Shortest-Path* program on all four metrics. Figure 7.4 shows the percentage of eventual best paths completed against time. The results show that *Hop-Count* has the fastest convergence time of 2.9 s, followed by *Latency* and *Reliability* in 3.5 s, and 3.9 s, respectively. *Random* has the worst convergence time of 5.5 s.

During program execution, the communication overhead incurred by all four queries shows a similar trend (Figure 7.3). Initially, the communication overhead increases as more and more paths (of increasing length) are derived. After it peaks at around $53\,K\,Bps$ per-node, the communication overhead decreases, as fewer and fewer optimal paths are left to be derived. In terms of aggregate communication overhead, *Random* incurs the most overhead (18.2 MB), while *Hop-Count, Latency*

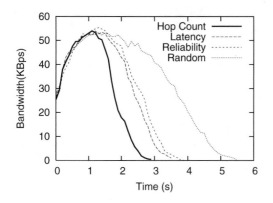

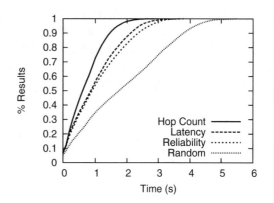

Figure 7.3: Per-node bandwidth (KBps) with Aggregate Selections.

Figure 7.4: Results over time (seconds) with Aggregate Selections.

and *Reliability* use 9.1 MB, 12.0 MB and 12.8 MB, respectively. The relatively poor performance of *Random* is due to the lack of correlation between the metric and network latency, leading to a greater tendency for out-of-order arrival of path tuples that results in less effective use of aggregate selection, translating to more messaging overhead and delays.

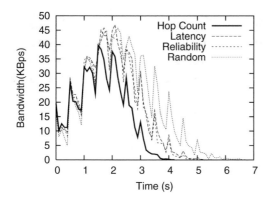

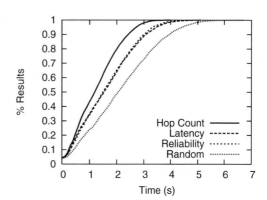

Figure 7.5: Per-node bandwidth (KBps) with periodic aggregate selections.

Figure 7.6: Results over time (seconds) with periodic aggregate selections.

The results in Figures 7.5 and 7.6 illustrate the effectiveness of the *periodic aggregate selections* approach, as described in Section 7.1.1, where the wait period is set to 500 ms. In particular, this approach reduces the bandwidth usage of *Hop-Count*, *Latency*, *Reliability* and *Random* by 19%,

15%, 23% and 34%, respectively. *Random* shows the greatest reduction in communication overhead, demonstrating the effectiveness of this technique for improving the performance of queries on metrics that are uncorrelated with network delay.

7.4.2   MAGIC SETS AND PREDICATE REORDERING

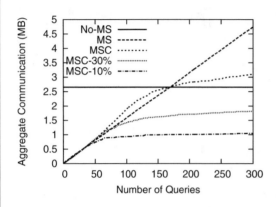 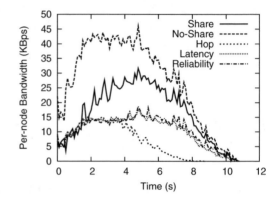

Figure 7.7: Aggregate communication overhead (MB) with and without magic sets and caching.

Figure 7.8: Per-node bandwidth (KBps) for message sharing (300 ms delay).

The next experiment studies the effectiveness of combining the use of magic sets and predicate reordering for lowering communication overhead when the requested shortest paths are constrained by randomly chosen sources and destinations. The workload consists of queries that request source-to-destination paths based on the *Hop-Count* metric. Each query executes the *Magic-Shortest-Path* program (Section 7.1.2).

Figure 7.7 shows the aggregate communication overhead as the number of queries increases. The *No-MS* line represents our baseline, and shows the communication overhead in the absence of rewrites (this essentially reduces to computing all-pairs least-hop-count). The *MS* line shows the communication overhead when running the program optimized with magic sets, but without any sharing across queries. When there are few queries, the communication overhead of *MS* is significantly lower than that of *NO-MS*. As the number of queries increases, the communication overhead of *MS* increases linearly, exceeding *No-MS* after 170 queries.

In addition, Figure 7.7 also illustrates the effectiveness of caching (Section 7.2). The *MSC* line shows the aggregate communication overhead for magic sets with caching. For fewer than 170 queries, there is some overhead associated with caching. This is due to false positive cache hits, where a cache result does not contribute to computing the eventual shortest path. However, as the number of queries increases, the overall cache hit rate improves, resulting in a dramatic reduction of bandwidth. When limiting the choice of destination nodes to 30% (*MSC-30%*) and 10% (*MSC-*

10%), the communication overhead levels of at 1.8 MB, and 1 MB, respectively. The smaller the set of requested destinations, the higher the cache hit rate, and the greater the opportunity for sharing across different queries.

7.4.3   OPPORTUNISTIC MESSAGE SHARING

The next experiment studies the impact of performing opportunistic message sharing across concurrent queries that have some correlation in the messages being sent. Figure 7.8 shows per-node bandwidth usage for running the queries on different metrics concurrently. To facilitate sharing, each outbound tuple is delayed by 500 ms in anticipation of possible sharing opportunities. The *Latency*, *Reliability* and *Random* lines show the bandwidth usage of each query individually. The *No-Share* line shows the total aggregate bandwidth of these three queries without sharing. The *Share* line shows the aggregate bandwidth usage with sharing. The results clearly demonstrate the potential effectiveness of message sharing, which reduces the peak of the per-node communication overhead from 46 KBps to 31 KBps, and the total communication overhead by 39%.

7.4.4   SUMMARY OF OPTIMIZATIONS

The evaluation results are summarized as follows.

1. The aggregate selections optimization indeed reduces communication overhead. Using *periodic aggregate selections* reduces this overhead further.

2. The use of magic sets and predicate reordering reduces communication overhead when only a limited number of paths are queried.

3. Multi-query sharing techniques such as reusing previously computed results and opportunistic result caching demonstrate the potential to reduce communication overhead when there are several concurrent queries.

7.5   SUMMARY

This chapter applies a variety of query optimizations to declarative networks. The use of traditional query optimizations is explored, and new optimizations motivated by the distributed setting are proposed. The chapter demonstrates that declarative networks are amenable to automatic optimizations, and showed that many of these optimizations can improve the performance of declarative networks substantially. In addition, the effectiveness of several of our optimization techniques are validated on the Emulab testbed.

This chapter reveals surprising relationships between network optimizations and query optimizations, e.g., a wired protocol can be translated to a wireless protocol by applying the standard database optimizations of magic sets rewrite and predicate reordering. This suggests that these protocols are more similar than they are often made out to be. Recent work [Liu et al., 2009a, 2011a] has leveraged these connections between network optimizations and query optimizations, to propose a declarative framework for adaptive hybrid wireless ad-hoc network routing protocols.

CHAPTER 8

Recent Advances in Declarative Networking

This chapter presents recent advances in declarative networking. In recent years, research in declarative networking has evolved beyond its original roots as a framework for rapid prototyping, towards one that serves as an important bridge connecting formal theories for reasoning about protocol correctness and actual implementations. The ability to bridge this gap is a major step forward compared to traditional approaches in which formal specifications, proof of protocol correctness and implementations are decoupled from one another; this decoupling leads to increased development time, error prone implementations, and tedious debugging.

This chapter is organized as follows. Section 8.1 describes language extensions of declarative networking. Sections 8.2-8.5 present recent work aimed at addressing four significant challenges in distributed systems: generating safe routing implementations (Section 8.2), securing distributed systems (Section 8.3), debugging distributed systems (Section 8.4), and optimizing distributed systems (Section 8.5).

8.1 LANGUAGE EXTENSIONS

In the original NDlog language, predicates are allowed to be declared as *soft-state* with lifetimes. In the extreme case, *event predicates* form transient tables which are used as input to rules but are not stored. To support wireless broadcast [Liu et al., 2009a, 2011a, Muthukumar et al., 2009a], we have introduced a *broadcast location specifier* denoted by @* which causes a tuple to be broadcast to all nodes within wireless range of the node on which the rule is executed. In order to support network functionality composition and code reuse, *Composable Virtual Views* [Mao et al., 2008] define rule groups that perform a specific functionality when executed together. These extensions offer different levels of declarativity [Mao, 2009] to meet various application demands.

The meaning of a NDlog program is defined to be the behavior and output obtained by running the program through PSN evaluation [Loo et al., 2006, Nigam et al., 2011]. The *Dedalus* [Alvaro et al., 2009, Hellerstein, 2010] language is similar to NDlog, except its behavior and output is defined in terms of a model-theoretic semantics. Dedalus also allows users to write rules that mutate state.

Dedalus takes base Datalog, and adds an integer *timestamp* field to every tuple. State update is expressed as locally-stratified recursion through negation. Message delay and re-ordering is captured by requiring all rules to derive non-local tuples at some non-deterministic future timestamp.

Dedalus uses Saccà and Zaniolo's `choice` construct [Saccà and Zaniolo, 1990] to model this non-determinism, which manifests itself in multiple *stable models* [Gelfond and Lifschitz, 1988]—one model for each possible choice of timestamp.

An interesting question is to what extent the behavior and output of the program is "well-behaved." The *CALM Conjecture* [Hellerstein, 2010] states that monotonic *coordination-free* Dedalus programs are *eventually consistent*, and non-monotonic programs are eventually consistent when instrumented with appropriate coordination. Recently, Ameloot et al. explored Hellerstein's CALM conjecture using relational transducers [Ameloot et al., 2011]. They proved that monotonic first order queries are exactly the set of queries that can be computed in a coordination-free fashion in their transducer formalism. Their work uses some different assumptions than traditional declarative networking—for example, they assume that all messages sent by a node are multicast to a fixed set of neighbors, whereas NDlog permits arbitrary unicast.

8.2   GENERATING SAFE ROUTING IMPLEMENTATIONS

The *Formally Verifiable Routing (FVR)* project addresses a long-standing challenge in networking research: bridging the gap between formal routing theories and actual implementations. The application of declarative networking is especially useful here, serving as an intermediary layer between high-level formal specifications of the network design and low-level implementations.

8.2.1   FORMALLY SAFE ROUTING TOOLKIT

The *Formally Safe Routing (FSR)* toolkit [Wang et al., 2011] attempts to bridge this gap in the context of interdomain routing by unifying research in routing algebras [Griffin and Sobrinho, 2005] with declarative networking to produce provably correct distributed implementations. Specifically, FSR automates the process of analyzing routing configurations expressed in algebra for safety (i.e., convergence) using the Yices SMT solver [Yices], and automatically compiles routing algebra into declarative routing implementations.

To enable an evaluation of protocol dynamics and convergence time, FSR uses an extended routing algebra [Wang et al., 2011] to automatically generate a distributed routing-protocol implementation that matches the policy configuration—avoiding the time-consuming and error-prone task of manually creating an implementation. FSR generates a provably correct translation to a NDlog specification, which is then executed using the RapidNet declarative networking engine.

The choice of NDlog as the basis for FSR is motivated by the following. First, the declarative features of NDlog allow for straightforward translation from the routing algebra to NDlog programs. Second, NDlog enables a variety of routing protocols and overlay networks to be specified in a natural and concise manner. Given that NDlog specifications are orders of magnitude less code than imperative implementations, this makes possible a clean and concise proof (via logical inductions) of the correctness of the generated NDlog programs with regard to safety. The compact specifications also make it easy to incorporate alternative routing mechanisms to the basic path-vector protocol, as demonstrated in [Wang et al., 2011]. Finally, when compiled and executed, these declarative protocols perform efficiently relative to imperative routing implementations.

A recent prototype demonstration [Ren et al., 2011] shows how FSR can detect problems in an AS's iBGP configuration (using realistic topologies and policies). FSR has also been used to prove sufficient conditions for BGP safety and empirically evaluate protocol dynamics and convergence time.

FSR serves two important communities. For researchers, FSR automates important parts of the design process and provides a common framework for describing, evaluating, and comparing new safety guidelines. For network operators, FSR automates the analysis of internal router (iBGP) and border gateway (eBGP) configurations for safety violations. For both communities, FSR automatically generates realistic protocol implementations to evaluate real network configurations (e.g., to study convergence time) prior to actual deployment.

8.2.2   DECLARATIVE NETWORK VERIFICATION

In addition to the FSR toolkit, theorem proving techniques have been used for verifying declarative networking programs. The *DNV (Declarative Network Verification)* [Wang et al., 2009] toolkit demonstrates the feasibility of automatically compiling declarative networking programs written in NDlog into formal specifications recognizable by a theorem prover (e.g., , PVS [PVS]) for verification. Unlike model checkers, DNV can express properties beyond the temporal properties to which most model-checking techniques are restricted. It also avoids the state exploration problem inherent in model checking. Theorem proving techniques are also sound and complete: once a property is verified, it holds for all instances of the protocol. Moreover, modern theorem provers come with powerful proof engines that support a large portion of automated proof exploration, enabling the proof of non-trivial theorems with relatively modest human effort.

8.3   SECURING DISTRIBUTED SYSTEMS

The *Declarative Secure Distributed Systems (DS2)* platform provides high-level programming abstractions for implementing secure distributed systems, achieved by unifying declarative networking and logic-based access control specifications [DeTreville, 2002]. DS2 has a wide range of applications, including reconfigurable trust management [Marczak et al., 2009], secure distributed data processing [Marczak et al., 2010], and tunable anonymity [Sherr et al., 2010].

DS2 is motivated in part by the observation that distributed trust management languages share similarities with both data integration languages and the distributed Datalog languages proposed for declarative networking. These languages support the notion of *context* (location) to identify *components* (nodes) in distributed systems. The commonalities between these languages indicate that ideas and methods from the database community are also applicable to processing security policies, suggesting the unification of these declarative languages to create an integrated system.

The DS2 system is currently available for download [RapidNet].

8.3.1   SECURE NETWORK DATALOG

The *Secure Network Datalog (SeNDlog)* language [Zhou et al., 2009] unifies NDlog and logic-based languages for access control in distributed systems. SeNDlog enables network routing, information systems, and security policies to be specified and implemented within a common declarative framework. To execute SeNDlog programs, existing distributed recursive query processing techniques have been extended to incorporate secure communication among untrusted nodes.

In SeNDlog, a set of rules and the associated tuples are bounded to reside at a particular node. This is achieved at the top level for each rule (or set of rules), for example by specifying:

```
At N,
   r1 p :- p1, p2 , ..., pn.
   r2 p1 :- p2, p3 , ..., pn.
```

The above rules `r1` and `r2` are in the context of `N`, where `N` is either a variable or a constant representing the principal where the rules reside. If `N` is a variable, it will be instantiated with local information upon rule installation. In a trusted distributed environment, `N` simply represents the network address of a node: either a physical address (e.g., an IP address) or a logical address (e.g., an overlay identifier). In a multi-user multi-layered network environment where multiple users and overlay networks may reside on the same physical node, `N` can include the user name and an overlay network identifier. This is unlike declarative networking in which location specifiers denote physical IP address.

SeNDlog allows different principals or contexts to communicate via import and export of tuples. The communication serves two purposes: (1) maintenance messages as part of a network protocol's updates on routing tables, and (2) distributed derivation of security decisions. Imported tuples from a principal `N` are automatically quoted using "`N says`" to differentiate them from local tuples. During the evaluation of SeNDlog rules, derived tuples are allowed to be communicated among contexts via the use of *import predicates* and *export predicates*:

- An *import predicate* is of the form "`N says p`" in a rule body, where principal `N` asserts the predicate p.

- An *export predicate* is of the form "`N says p@X`" in a rule head, where principal `N` exports the predicate p to the context of principal `X`. Here, `X` can be a constant or a variable. If `X` is a variable, in order to make bottom-up evaluation efficient, it is further required that the variable `X` occur in the rule body. As a shorthand, "`N says`" can be omitted if `N` is the principal where the rule resides.

By exporting tuples only to specified principals, the use of export predicates ensures confidentiality and prevents information leakage. With the above definitions, a SeNDlog rule is a Datalog rule where the rule body can include import predicates and the rule head can be an export predicate.

To illustrate SeNDlog using an example, consider a secure implementation of the declarative path vector protocol (shown in Figure 8.1). At every node Z, this program takes as input `neighbor(Z,X)` tuples that contain all neighbors X for Z. The program generates `route(Z,X,P)` tuples, each of which stores the path P from source Z to destination X. The basic protocol specification is similar to the all-pairs reachable example presented in Section 2.2, with additional predicates for computing the actual path using the `f_concat` function which prepends neighbor X to the input path P.

The input `carryTraffic` and `acceptRoute` tables, respectively, represent the export and import policies of node Z. Each `carryTraffic(Z,X,Y)` tuple represents the fact that node Z is willing to serve all network traffic on behalf of node X to node Y, and each `acceptRoute(Z,Y,X)` tuple represents the fact that node Z will accept a route from node X to node Y. A more complex version of this protocol will have additional rules that derive `carryTraffic` and `acceptRoute`, avoid path cycles and also derive shortest paths with the least hop count.

The path-vector protocol is used for inter-domain routing over the Internet and is known to be vulnerable to a variety of attacks due to the lack of mechanisms for verifying the authenticity and authorization of routing control traffic. One potential solution is to authenticate every routing control message, as proposed for Secure BGP [S-BGP].

At Z,

z1 route(Z,X,P) :- neighbor(Z,X), P=f_initPath(Z,X).

z2 route(Z,Y,P) :- X says advertise(Y,P), acceptRoute(Z,X,Y).

z3 advertise(Y,P1)@X :- neighbor(Z,X), route(Z,Y,P),
                       carryTraffic(Z,X,Y), P1=f_concat(X,P).

Figure 8.1: SeNDlog specification of the secure path-vector protocol.

In this example program, such authentication can be naturally specified via the use of "says" to ensure that all `advertise` tuples are verified by the recipients for authenticity. Rule z1 takes as input `neighbor(Z,X)` tuples, and computes all the single hop `route(Z,X,P)` containing the path [Z,X] from node Z to X. Rules z2 and z3 compute routes of increasing hop counts. Upon receiving an `advertise(Y,P)` tuple from X, Z uses rule z2 to decide whether to accept the route advertisement based on its local `acceptRoute` table. If the route is accepted, a `route` tuple is derived locally, and this results in the generation of an `advertise` tuple which is further exported by node Z via rule z3 to some of its neighbors X as determined by the policies stored in the local `carryTraffic` table.

SeNDlog is able to compactly specify a variety of secure distributed protocols. Zhou et al. [2009] has demonstrated, for example, the use of SeNDlog for performing secure distributed joins and securing distributed hash tables [Balakrishnan et al., 2003].

8.3.2   RECONFIGURABLE SECURITY

Although one can achieve a high level of security using a "one-size-fits-all" solution with fixed constructs like says, an *extensible trust management* framework where users can write and reconfigure their own constructs like says is applicable to a much broader range of settings. For example, programmers could customize the security protocols used by their application based on the execution environment without modifying the application logic. *LBTrust* [Marczak et al., 2009] extends SeNDlog to support user-defined security constructs that can be customized and composed in a declarative fashion. To validate these ideas in a production system, this extension has been implemented in the LogicBlox [LogicBlox Inc.] system, an emerging commercial Datalog-based platform for enterprise software systems.

In addition, LogicBlox is enhanced to support *meta-rules* [Condie et al., 2008]—Datalog rules that operate on the rules of the program as input, and produce new rules as output—and *meta-constraints*—Datalog constraints that restrict the allowable rules in the program. Security constructs are written using these two ingredients. For example, the says construct would consist of meta-rules that rewrite the program to perform signing of all exported messages, and constraints that ensure that all imported messages have valid signatures. In LBTrust, a variety of security primitives for authentication, confidentiality, integrity, speaks-for, and restricted delegation can be supported. Based on these primitives, several existing distributed trust management systems (e.g., Binder [DeTreville, 2002], SD3 [Jim, 2001], Delegation Logic [Li et al., 2003], and SeNDlog) can be implemented in LBTrust.

A follow-up to LBTrust is the *SecureBlox* [Marczak et al., 2010] system, which restricts the use of meta-programming to make it a fully static, compile-time operation. SecureBlox includes support for physical distribution, and looks at performance-security tradeoffs between different constructs in distributed systems. Similar to LBTrust, SecureBlox allows meta-programmability for compile-time code generation based on the security requirements and trust policies of the deployed environment.

While security is specifically studied in the LBTrust and SecureBlox work, the general pattern of using meta-programming to decompose a logic program into different aspects representing crosscutting concerns is more broadly applicable.

8.3.3   APPLICATION-AWARE ANONYMITY

To further illustrate the feasibility of these methods and technologies for the development of secure distributed systems, the *Application-Aware Anonymity (A^3)* system [A3, Sherr et al., 2010] is a distributed peer-to-peer service that provides high-performance anonymity *for the masses*. A^3 uses SeNDlog for implementing an extensible policy engine for customizing its relay selection and instantiation strategies. A^3 allows applications to construct anonymous Onion [Goldschlag et al., 1999] paths that adhere to application specific constraints (e.g., end-to-end latency). Unlike existing anonymity systems that construct paths according to predefined criteria, A^3 enables applications to specify the requirements of their anonymous paths. For example, anonymized Voice-over-IP services can request paths with low latency and modest bandwidth requirements, while streaming

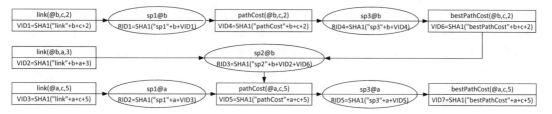

Figure 8.2: The provenance graph of the tuple `bestPathCost(@a,c,5)` derived from the execution of the MinCost program. Ovals represent rule execution vertexes and rectangles denote tuple vertexes.

video broadcasts can request high bandwidth anonymous paths without regard for latency. A^3 is open-source and available for download [A3].

8.4   DEBUGGING DISTRIBUTED SYSTEMS

In the context of distributed systems, it is very common for system administrators to perform analysis tasks that essentially amount to *network provenance* [Zhou et al., 2008, 2010] queries. For example, they might ask diagnostic queries to determine the root cause of a malfunction, forensic queries to identify the source of an intrusion, or profiling queries to find the reason for suboptimal performance.

The *NetTrails* [Zhou et al., 2010, 2011c] system is a declarative platform for incrementally maintaining, interactively navigating, and querying network provenance in a distributed system. During the system execution, NetTrails incrementally maintains provenance information using Rapid-Net as its distributed query engine. NetTrails offers a unifying framework, as both maintenance and querying functionalities are specified as NDlog programs.

NetTrails consists of two subcomponents: First, a *maintenance engine* takes as input either NDlog programs or input/output dependencies captured from legacy applications, and then incrementally computes and maintains network provenance information as distributed relational tables. Second, a *distributed query engine* executes user-customizable provenance queries that are evaluated across multiple nodes. Legacy systems are supported either by modifying the application's source code to explicitly report provenance, or by using an external specification of the application's protocol to derive provenance information by observing a node's inputs and outputs [Zhou et al., 2011b].

8.4.1   NETWORK PROVENANCE MODEL

In NetTrails, the provenance graph is internally maintained as relational tables which are distributed and partitioned across all nodes in the network. Network provenance is modeled as an acyclic graph $G(V, E)$. The vertex set V consists of *tuple vertices* and *rule execution vertices*. Each tuple vertex in the graph is either a base tuple or a computation result, and each rule execution vertex represents an instance of a rule execution given a set of input tuples. The edge set E represents dataflows between tuples and rule execution vertices.

To illustrate, consider an example network consisting of three nodes a, b and c connected by three bi-directional links (a,b), (a,c) and (b,c) with costs 3, 5 and 2 respectively. The following three-rule MinCost program found in Figure 8.3 computes the minimal path cost between each pair of nodes.

---

sp1 pathCost(@S,D,C) :- link(@S,D,C).
sp2 pathCost(@S,D,C1+C2) :- link(@Z,S,C1), bestPathCost(@Z,D,C2).
sp3 bestPathCost(@S,D,MIN<C>) :- pathCost(@S,D,C).

Figure 8.3: The MinCost protocol.

Figure 8.2 shows the provenance for a specific derived tuple bestPathCost(@a,c,5), based on the dependency logic captured by the MinCost program. For instance, the figure shows that bestPathCost(@a,c,5) is generated from rule sp3 at node a taking pathCost(@a,c,5) as the input. To trace further, pathCost(@a,c,5) has two derivations: the locally derivable one-hop path $a \rightarrow c$ and the two-hop path $a \rightarrow b \rightarrow c$ that requires a distributed join at b.

8.4.2   DISTRIBUTED MAINTENANCE AND QUERYING

Given the adoption of a declarative networking engine, data dependencies are explicitly captured in derivation rules.[1] The provenance maintenance in a dynamic system execution can be performed in a straightforward manner: an automatic rule rewrite algorithm takes as input a set of derivation rules, and outputs a modified program that contains additional rules for capturing the provenance information. These additional rules define network provenance in terms of views over base and derived tuples. As the network protocol executes and updates network state, views are incrementally recomputed.

Once generated, network provenance can be queried by issuing distributed queries. Since provenance information is distributed across nodes, query execution performs a traversal of the provenance graphs in a distributed fashion.

NetTrails allows users to customize the provenance queries. For instance, users can query for a tuple's lineage, the set of nodes that have been involved in the derivation of a given tuples, and/or the total number of alternative derivations. To reduce querying overhead, NetTrails adopts a set of optimization techniques [Zhou et al., 2010], including caching previously queried results, leveraging alternative tree traversal orders, and performing threshold-based pruning.

Figure 8.4 shows an example execution of a demonstration [Zhou et al., 2011c] that highlights the provenance of the system state (captured as tuples) for a running MinCost program. One may further issue customized provenance queries and visually inspect the progressive steps of the distributed querying.

---

[1]For legacy applications, the data dependencies (reported by the modified source code or inferred from the observed I/Os) can be formulated as derivation rules as well [Zhou et al., 2011b].

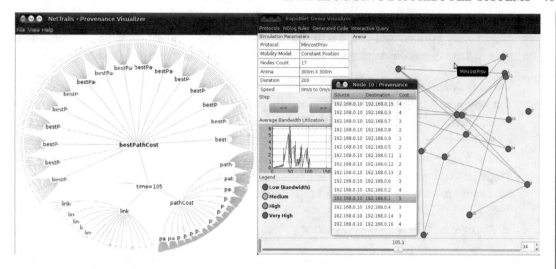

Figure 8.4: A screenshot of the NetTrails demonstration [Zhou et al., 2011c].

8.4.3   SECURITY AND TEMPORAL EXTENSIONS

NetTrails provides functionality required for richer provenance queries by adding: (i) new provenance models and maintenance strategies for capturing the time, distribution, and causality of updates in distributed systems [Zhou et al., 2011a], and (ii) novel query processing and optimization techniques for efficiently and securely answering queries at scale [Zhou et al., 2011b].

NetTrails explicitly captures *causality*: if some network state α depends on some other state β, and β is changed, the provenance of the *change* in α is attributable to the change in β. Additionally, since one of the potential use cases is forensics, NetTrails achieves strong *security guarantees* even in the presence of misbehaving and potentially malicious nodes. NetTrails utilizes *secure network provenance* [Zhou et al., 2011b] to provide the strong guarantee that either a returned provenance query is accurate and complete, or that a misbehaving node is identified with non-repudiable evidence against the node.

To demonstrate the capabilities of NetTrails's temporal and security extensions, a number of use cases of the NetTrails system have been developed.

- **Network Routing.** The *Border Gateway Protocol* (BGP) used for interdomain routing over the Internet is plagued by a variety of attacks and malfunctions. NetTrails has been applied to the Quagga BGP daemon [Quagga] and demonstrated how NetTrails enables a network administrator to determine why an entry from a routing table has disappeared. NetTrails is capable of detecting well-known BGP misconfigurations.

- **Distributed Hash Tables.** NetTrails has been applied to a declarative implementation of the Chord [Loo et al., 2005a] distributed hash table; no modifications are required to the Chord source code. NetTrails has the ability to detect a well-known attack against Chord in which the attacker gains control over a large fraction of the neighbors of a correct node, and is then able to drop or reroute messages to this node and prevent correct overlay operation.

- **Hadoop MapReduce.** Finally, NetTrails has been applied to Hadoop MapReduce [Hadoop]. Hadoop is manually instrumented to report provenance at the level of individual key-value pairs. The *WordCount* program written in Hadoop is used to reports the number of occurrences of each word in a 1.2 GB Wikipedia dataset. In this scenario, the provenance of a given (unlikely) key-value pair in the output is queried. NetTrails revealed that unexpected results might be attributed to a faulty or compromised map worker. More generally, NetTrails is able to identify the causes of suspicious MapReduce outputs.

8.5   OPTIMIZING DISTRIBUTED SYSTEMS

In distributed systems management, operators often configure system parameters that optimize performance objectives, given constraints in the deployment environment. Recent extensions to the original declarative networking framework has led to a declarative optimization platform that enables constraint optimization problems (COP) to be declaratively specified and incrementally executed in distributed systems.

Traditional COP implementation approaches use imperative languages such as C++ or Java and often result in cumbersome and error-prone programs that are difficult to maintain and customize. Moreover, due to scalability and management constraints imposed across administrative domains, it is often necessary to execute COP in a *distributed* setting in which multiple *local* solvers must coordinate with one another. Each local solver handles a portion of the whole problem, and they together achieve a global objective.

Central to the optimization platform is the integration of a *declarative networking engine* [Loo et al., 2009] with an off-the-shelf constraint solver [Gecode]. This platform has been applied to two use cases.

8.5.1   USE CASES: PUMA AND COPE

First, the *Policy-based Unified Multi-radio Architecture* (PUMA), a declarative constraint solving platform for optimizing wireless mesh networks. In PUMA, network operators can flexibly vary the choice of routing via adaptable *hybrid* routing protocols [Liu et al., 2011a]. The hybrid technique combines several existing protocols (e.g., , proactive, reactive, and epidemic) with specific criteria for determining when particular protocols are to be used. The hybrid compositional capabilities are particularly useful for routing in heterogeneous network settings in which application needs and network conditions keep changing over time. In addition, PUMA enables policies for *wireless channel selection* [Liu et al., 2012] to be declaratively specified and optimized; such policies may reduce network interference and maximize throughput while not violating constraints (for instance, refraining from channels owned exclusively by the primary users [Perich, 2007]).

Second, the *Cloud Orchestration Policy Engine* (COPE) [Liu et al., 2011b] uses the optimization framework to declaratively control the provisioning, configuration, management and decommissioning of cloud resource orchestration. COPE enables the automatic realization of customer service level agreements while simultaneously conforming to operational objectives of the cloud providers.

Beyond these two use cases, this platform has a wide-range of potential applications, including optimizing distributed systems for load balancing, robust routing, scheduling, and security.

8.5.2   COLOG LANGUAGE AND COMPILATION

The optimization platform uses the *Colog* declarative policy language. Colog allows operators to concisely model distributed system resources and formulate management decisions as declarative programs with specified goals and constraints. Compared to traditional imperative alternatives, Colog results in code that is smaller by orders of magnitude, and is easier to understand, debug and extend. Here, high-level intuitions of Colog are presented; a more comprehensive treatment of the language can be found here [Liu et al., 2011b, 2012].

- **Language extensions.** Based on NDlog, Colog extends traditional NDlog with constructs for expressing goals and constraints. Two reserved keywords—`goal` and `var`, respectively, specify the *optimization goal* and *variables* used by the constraint solver. *Constraint* rules of the form F1 -> F2, F3, ..., Fn denote that whenever F1 is true, then the rule body (F2 and F3 and ... and Fn) must also be true to satisfy the constraint. Unlike a Datalog rule which derives new values for a predicate, a constraint *restricts* a predicate's allowed values, hence representing an invariant that must be maintained at all times. These are used by the solver to limit the search space when computing the optimization goal. Using Colog, it is easy to customize policies simply by modifying the goals and constraints, and by adding additional derivation rules.

- **Distributed COP.** Colog is extended for execution in a distributed setting. At a high level, multiple solver nodes execute a *local* COP, and then iteratively exchange COP results with neighboring nodes until a stopping condition is reached. Similar to NDlog, in the distributed COP program, a location specifier @ denotes the source location of each corresponding tuple. This allows us to write rules in which the input data span multiple nodes—a convenient language construct for formulating distributed optimizations.

One of the interesting aspects of Colog, from a query processing standpoint, is the integration of RapidNet (an incremental bottom-up distributed Datalog evaluation engine) and Gecode (a top-down goal-oriented constraint solver). This integration allows us to implement a distributed solver that can perform incremental and distributed constraint optimizations.

To execute distributed COP rules, Colog uses RapidNet, which already provides a runtime environment for implementing these rules. At a high level, each distributed rule or constraint (with multiple distinct location specifiers) is rewritten using a *localization* rewrite [Loo et al., 2009] step. This transformation results in rule bodies that can be executed locally and rule heads that can be derived and sent across nodes. The beauty of this rewrite is that even if the original program expresses distributed properties and constraints, the rewrite process will realize multiple local COP operations at different nodes, and have the output of COP operations via derivations sent across nodes.

8.6   SUMMARY

This chapter focuses on the use of declarative networking for addressing four main challenges in the distributed systems development cycle: the generation of safe routing implementations, debugging, security and privacy, and optimizing distributed systems. In addition to the fast-prototyping capabilities brought by the orders of magnitude reduction in code size (compared to imperative implementation), recent advances explore the research opportunities enabled by the root of declarative networking in logic-based specification languages. It fundamentally eases the process of bridging formal analysis and implementation in practice, to allow automatic code-synthesis for provably correct implementation. In addition, the execution model of NDlog aligns naturally with how distributed systems execute in general, enabling an automated approach towards maintaining and querying state dependencies using network provenance.

CHAPTER 9

Conclusion

In Jim Gray's Turing Award Lecture [Gray, 2000], one of his grand challenges was the development of "automatic programming" techniques that would be: (a) 1000× easier for people to use, (b) directly compiled into working code, and (c) suitable for general purpose use. Butler Lampson reiterated the first two points in a subsequent invited article, but suggested that they might be more tractable in domain-specific settings [Lampson, 2003].

Declarative Networking has gone a long way towards Gray's vision, if only in the domain of network protocol implementation. On multiple occasions we have seen at least two orders of magnitude reduction in code size, with the reduced linecount producing qualitative improvements. In the case of Chord, a multi-thousand line C++ library was rewritten as a declarative program that fits on a single sheet of paper—a software artifact that can be studied and holistically understood by a programmer in a single sitting.

A high-level declarative language not only simplifies a programmer's work, but re-focuses the programming task on appropriately high-level issues. For example, declarative routing has demonstrated that discussions of routing in wired vs. wireless networks should not result in different protocols, but rather in different compiler optimizations for the same simple declaration, with the potential to be automatically blended into new hybrid strategies as networks become more diverse [Chu and Hellerstein, 2009, Liu et al., 2009a, Loo et al., 2005b]. This lifting of abstractions seems well suited to the increasing complexity of modern networking, introducing software malleability by minimizing the affordances for over-engineering solutions to specific settings.

Broadly, declarative networking have impacted the networking and database communities in the following ways. For the networking community, declarative networking has the potential to fundamentally alter the way networking protocols are designed, implemented and verified. For the database community, this research agenda has been a factor towards rekindling interest in recursive query research [Huang et al., 2011], and highlighting research opportunities at the intersection of data management and networking, and synergies available by intertwining the two within a single declarative framework.

Bibliography

A3. Application Aware Anonymity. http://a3.cis.upenn.edu/. Cited on page(s) 92, 93

Serge Abiteboul, Richard Hull, and Victor Vianu. *Foundations of Databases*. Addison-Wesley, 1995. Cited on page(s) 4, 53

Peter Alvaro, William Marczak, Neil Conway, Joseph M. Hellerstein, David Maier, and Russell C Sears. Dedalus: Datalog in Time and Space. Technical Report UCB/EECS-2009-173, Berkeley, CA, 2009. Cited on page(s) 87

Peter Alvaro, Tyson Condie, Neil Conway, Khaled Elmeleegy, Joseph M. Hellerstein, and Russell Sears. Boom Analytics: Exploring Data-Centric, Declarative Programming for the Cloud. In *Proc. 5th ACM SIGOPS/EuroSys European Conf. on Computer Systems*, pages 223–236, 2010. DOI: 10.1145/1755913.1755937 Cited on page(s) 2

Tom J. Ameloot, Frank Neven, and Jan Van den Bussche. Relational Transducers for Declarative Networking. In *Proc. 30th ACM SIGACT-SIGMOD-SIGART Symp. on Principles of Database Systems*, pages 283–292, 2011. DOI: 10.1145/1989284.1989321 Cited on page(s) 88

Faiz Arni, Kayliang Ong, Shalom Tsur, Haixun Wang, and Carlo Zaniolo. The Deductive Database System LDL++. *Theory & Practice of Logic Prog.*, 3(1):61–94, 2003. Cited on page(s) 16

Hari Balakrishnan, M. Frans Kaashoek, David Karger, Robert Morris, and Ion Stoica. Looking Up Data in P2P Systems. *Commun. ACM*, 46(2):43–48, 2003. DOI: 10.1145/606272.606299 Cited on page(s) 91

I. Balbin and K. Ramamohanarao. A Generalization of the Differential Approach to Recursive Query Evaluation. *J. Logic Programming*, 4(3):259–262, 1987. DOI: 10.1016/0743-1066(87)90004-5 Cited on page(s) 5, 29

Tony Ballardie, Paul Francis, and Jon Crowcroft. Core Based Trees (CBT): An Architecture for Scalable Inter-Domain Multicast Routing. In *Proc. ACM Int. Conf. on Data Communication*, pages 85–95, 1993. Cited on page(s) 52

Francois Bancilhon, David Maier, Yehoshua Sagiv, and Jeffrey D Ullman. Magic Sets and Other Strange Ways to Implement Logic Programs. In *Proc. 5th ACM SIGACT-SIGMOD Symp. on Principles of Database Systems*, pages 1–15, 1986. DOI: 10.1145/6012.15399 Cited on page(s) 5, 78

Catriel Beeri and Raghu Ramakrishnan. On the Power of Magic. In *Proc. 6th ACM SIGACT-SIGMOD-SIGART Symp. on Principles of Database Systems*, pages 269–284, 1987. DOI: 10.1145/28659.28689 Cited on page(s) 5, 78

Brian Bershad, Stefan Savage, Przemyslaw Pardyak, Emin Gun Sirer, David Becker, Marc Fiuczynski, Craig Chambers, and Susan Eggers. Extensibility, Safety and Performance in the SPIN Operating System. In *Proc. 15th ACM Symp. on Operating System Principles*, 1995. DOI: 10.1145/224057.224077 Cited on page(s) 4, 52

Diego Calvanese, Giuseppe De Giacomo, and Moshe Y. Vardi. Decidable Containment of Recursive Queries. In *Proc. 9th Int. Conf. on Database Theory*, pages 330–345, 2003. DOI: 10.1016/j.tcs.2004.10.031 Cited on page(s) 80

Xu Chen, Yun Mao, Z. Morley Mao, and Jacobus van der Merwe. Declarative Configuration Management for Complex and Dynamic Networks. In *Proc. Int. Conf. emerging Networking EXperiments and Technologies*, pages 1–12, 2010. DOI: 10.1145/1921168.1921176 Cited on page(s) 2

David Chu and Joseph Hellerstein. Automating Rendezvous and Proxy Selection in Sensor Networks. In *Proc. 8th Int. Symp. Information Proc. in Sensor Networks*, pages 73–84, 2009. Cited on page(s) 99

David Chu, Lucian Popa, Arsalan Tavakoli, Joseph M. Hellerstein, Philip Levis, Scott Shenker, and Ion Stoica. The Design and Implementation of a Declarative Sensor Network System. In *Proc. 5th Int. Conf. on Embedded Networked Sensor Systems*, pages 175–188, 2007. DOI: 10.1145/1322263.1322281 Cited on page(s) 2

Yang-Hua Chu, Sanjay G. Rao, and Hui Zhang. A Case for End System Multicast. In *Proc. 2000 ACM SIGMETRICS Int. Conf. on Measurement and Modeling of Computer Systems*, pages 1–12, 2000. DOI: 10.1145/339331.339337 Cited on page(s) 5, 59, 60, 64

David D. Clark. The design philosophy of the DARPA internet protocols. In *Proc. ACM Int. Conf. on Data Communication*, pages 106–114, 1988. DOI: 10.1145/52325.52336 Cited on page(s) 13

T. Clausen and P. Jacquet. Optimized link state routing protocol (olsr). 2003. RFC 3626 (Experimental). Cited on page(s) 27

Edgar F. Codd. A Relational Model of Data for Large Shared Data Banks. *Commun. ACM*, 13(6): 377–387, 1970. DOI: 10.1145/362384.362685 Cited on page(s) 77

Tyson Condie, Joseph M. Hellerstein, Petros Maniatis, Sean Rhea, and Timothy Roscoe. Finally, a Use for Componentized Transport Protocols. In *Proc. 4th Workshop on Hot Topics in Networks*, pages 43–48, 2005. Cited on page(s) 23, 24

Tyson Condie, David Chu, Joseph M. Hellerstein, and Petros Maniatis. Evita Raced: Metacompilation for Declarative Networks. In *Proc. 34th Int. Conf. on Very Large Data Bases*, pages 1153–1165, 2008. DOI: 10.1145/1453856.1453978 Cited on page(s) 92

S. Deering and D. R. Cheriton. Multicast Routing in Datagram Internetworks and Extended LANs. *ACM Trans. Comp. Syst.*, 8(2):85–111, 1990. DOI: 10.1145/78952.78953 Cited on page(s) 60

John DeTreville. Binder: A Logic-Based Security Language. In *Proc. 23rd IEEE Symp. Security and Privacy*, pages 105–113, 2002. DOI: 10.1109/SECPRI.2002.1004365 Cited on page(s) 89, 92

David J. DeWitt, Robert H. Gerber, Goetz Graefe, Michael L. Heytens, Krishna B. Kumar, and M. Muralikrishna. GAMMA - A High Performance Dataflow Database Machine. In *Proc. 12th Int. Conf. on Very Large Data Bases*, pages 228–237, 1986. Cited on page(s) 23

Emulab. Network Emulation Testbed. http://www.emulab.net/. Cited on page(s) 72, 73

Nick Feamster, Hari Balakrishnan, Jennifer Rexford, Aman Shaikh, and Jacobus van der Merwe. The Case for Separating Routing From Routers. In *Proc. ACM SIGCOMM Workshop on Future Directions in Network Architecture*, pages 5–12, 2004. DOI: 10.1145/1016707.1016709 Cited on page(s) 47

Filippo Furfaro, Sergio Greco, Sumit Ganguly, and Carlo Zaniolo. Pushing Extrema Aggregates to Optimize Logic Queries. *Info. Sys.*, 27(5):321–343, 2002. DOI: 10.1016/S0306-4379(02)00006-6 Cited on page(s) 5, 77

Gecode. Gecode constraint development environment. http://www.gecode.org/. Cited on page(s) 96

Michael Gelfond and Vladimir Lifschitz. The Stable Model Semantics For Logic Programming. In *Proc. Int. Logic Prog. Conf. and Symp.*, pages 1070–1080, 1988. Cited on page(s) 88

Harjot Gill, Taher Saeed, Qiong Fei, Zhuoyao Zhang, and Boon Thau Loo. An Open-source and Declarative Approach Towards Teaching Large-scale Networked Systems Programming. In *Proc. ACM SIGCOMM Workshop on Education*, pages 1–6, 2011. Cited on page(s) 2

David Goldschlag, Michael Reed, and Paul Syverson. Onion Routing. *Commun. ACM*, 42(2):39–41, 1999. DOI: 10.1145/293411.293443 Cited on page(s) 92

Goetz Graefe. Encapsulation of Parallelism in the Volcano Query Processing System. In *Proc. ACM SIGMOD Int. Conf. on Management of Data*, pages 102–111, 1990. DOI: 10.1145/93605.98720 Cited on page(s) 23, 32

Jim Gray. What Next? A Few Remaining Problems in Information Technology, SIGMOD Conference 1999, ACM Turing Award Lecture, Video. *ACM SIGMOD Digital Symposium Collection*, 2(2), 2000. Cited on page(s) 99

Timothy G. Griffin and Joao Luis Sobrinho. Metarouting. In *Proc. ACM Int. Conf. on Data Communication*, pages 1–12, 2005. DOI: 10.1145/1090191.1080094 Cited on page(s) 88

GT-ITM. Modelling topology of large networks. http://www.cc.gatech.edu/projects/gtitm/. DOI: 10.1098/rsta.2008.0008 Cited on page(s) 55

Ashish Gupta, Inderpal Singh Mumick, and V. S. Subrahmanian. Maintaining Views Incrementally. In *Proc. ACM SIGMOD Int. Conf. on Management of Data*, pages 157–166, 1993. DOI: 10.1145/170036.170066 Cited on page(s) 17, 37, 55

Zygmunt J. Haas. A New Routing Protocol for the Reconfigurable Wireless Networks. In *Proc. IEEE Int. Conf. on Universal Personal Communications*, pages 562–566, 1997. DOI: 10.1109/ICUPC.1997.627227 Cited on page(s) 82

Hadoop. Apeche hadoop project. http://hadoop.apache.org/. Cited on page(s) 96

Mark Handley, Eddie Kohler, Atanu Ghosh, Orion Hodson, and Pavlin Radoslavov. Designing Extensible IP Router Software. In *Proc. 2nd USENIX Symp. on Networked Systems Design & Implementation*, pages 189–202, 2005. Cited on page(s) 23, 45

Joseph M. Hellerstein. Declarative Imperative: Experiences and Conjectures in Distributed Logic. *ACM SIGMOD Rec.*, 39(1):5–19, 2010. DOI: 10.1145/1860702.1860704 Cited on page(s) 87, 88

Shan Shan Huang, Todd J. Green, and Boon Thau Loo. Datalog and Emerging Applications: An Interactive Tutorial. In *Proc. ACM SIGMOD Int. Conf. on Management of Data*, pages 1213–1216, 2011. DOI: 10.1145/1989323.1989456 Cited on page(s) 99

Ryan Huebsch, Brent Chun, Joseph Hellerstein, Boon Thau Loo, Petros Maniatis, Timothy Roscoe, Scott Shenker, Ion Stoica, and Aydan R. Yumerefendi. The Architecture of PIER: an Internet-Scale Query Processor. In *Proc. 2nd Biennial Conf. on Innovative Data Systems Research*, pages 28–43, 2005. Cited on page(s) 23, 24

Trevor Jim. SD3: A Trust Management System With Certified Evaluation. In *Proc. 22nd IEEE Symp. Security and Privacy*, pages 106–115, 2001. DOI: 10.1109/SECPRI.2001.924291 Cited on page(s) 92

David B Johnson and David A Maltz. Dynamic Source Routing in Ad Hoc Wireless Networks. In *Mobile Computing*, pages 153–181. 1996. DOI: 10.1007/978-0-585-29603-6_5 Cited on page(s) 27, 50, 79

Eddie Kohler, Robert Morris, Benjie Chen, John Jannotti, and M. Frans Kaashoek. The Click Modular Router. *ACM Trans. Comp. Syst.*, 18(3):263–297, 2000. DOI: 10.1145/354871.354874 Cited on page(s) 23, 25, 33

Ravi Krishnamurthy, Raghu Ramakrishnan, and Oded Shmueli. A Framework for Testing Safety and Effective Computability. *J. Comp. and System Sci.*, 52(1):100–124, 1996. DOI: 10.1006/jcss.1996.0009 Cited on page(s) 4, 53

Butler Lampson. Getting Computers to Understand. *J. ACM*, 50(1):70–72, 2003. DOI: 10.1145/602382.602404 Cited on page(s) 99

Ninghui Li, Benjamin N. Grosof, and Joan Feigenbaum. Delegation Logic: A Logic-based Approach to Distributed Authorization. *ACM Trans. Info. and Sys. Security*, 6(1):128–171, 2003. DOI: 10.1145/605434.605438 Cited on page(s) 92

Changbin Liu, Rick Correa, Xiaozhou Li, Prithwish Basu, Boon Thau Loo, and Yun Mao. Declarative Policy-based Adaptive MANET Routing. pages 354–363, 2009a. DOI: 10.1109/ICNP.2009.5339669 Cited on page(s) 26, 85, 87, 99

Changbin Liu, Richardo Correa, Xiaozhou Li, Prithwish Basu, Boon Thau Loo, and Yun Mao. Declarative Policy-based Adaptive Mobile Ad Hoc Networking. *IEEE/ACM Trans. Networking*, 2011a. DOI: 10.1109/TNET.2011.2165851 Cited on page(s) 2, 26, 85, 87, 96

Changbin Liu, Boon Thau Loo, and Yun Mao. Declarative Automated Cloud Resource Orchestration. In *Proc. ACM Symp. on Cloud Computing*, pages 1–8, 2011b. DOI: 10.1145/2038916.2038942 Cited on page(s) 97

Changbin Liu, Ricardo Correa, Harjot Gill, Tanveer Gill, Xiaozhou Li, Shivkumar Muthukumar, Taher Saeed, Boon Thau Loo, and Prithwish Basu. PUMA: Policy-based Unified Multi-radio Architecture for Agile Mesh Networking. In *Proc. Int. Conf. on Communication Systems and Networks*, pages 1–12, 2012. Cited on page(s) 2, 25, 96, 97

Mengmeng Liu, Nicholas Taylor, Wenchao Zhou, Zachary Ives, and Boon Thau Loo. Recursive Computation of Regions and Connectivity in Networks. In *Proc. 25th Int. Conf. on Data Engineering*, pages 1108–1119, 2009b. DOI: 10.1109/ICDE.2009.36 Cited on page(s) 40

LogicBlox Inc. http://www.logicblox.com/. Cited on page(s) 92

Boon Thau Loo. *The Design and Implementation of Declarative Networks*. PhD thesis, University of California, Berkeley, Berkeley, CA, 2006. Cited on page(s) xv, 34, 36, 40

Boon Thau Loo, Tyson Condie, Joseph M. Hellerstein, Petros Maniatis, Timothy Roscoe, and Ion Stoica. Implementing Declarative Overlays. In *Proc. 20th ACM Symp. on Operating System Principles*, pages 75–90, 2005a. DOI: 10.1145/1095809.1095818 Cited on page(s) 1, 95

Boon Thau Loo, Joseph M. Hellerstein, Ion Stoica, and Raghu Ramakrishnan. Declarative Routing: Extensible Routing with Declarative Queries. In *Proc. ACM Int. Conf. on Data Communication*, pages 289–300, 2005b. DOI: 10.1145/1090191.1080126 Cited on page(s) 1, 99

Boon Thau Loo, Tyson Condie, Minos Garofalakis, David E. Gay, Joseph M. Hellerstein, Petros Maniatis, Raghu Ramakrishnan, Timothy Roscoe, and Ion Stoica. Declarative Networking: Language, Execution and Optimization. In *Proc. ACM SIGMOD Int. Conf. on Management of Data*, pages 97–108, 2006. DOI: 10.1145/1142473.1142485 Cited on page(s) 1, 87

Boon Thau Loo, Tyson Condie, Minos Garofalakis, David E. Gay, Joseph M. Hellerstein, Petros Maniatis, Raghu Ramakrishnan, Timothy Roscoe, and Ion Stoica. Declarative Networking. *Commun. ACM*, 52(11):87–95, 2009. DOI: 10.1145/1592761.1592785 Cited on page(s) 1, 96, 97

Yun Mao. On the Declarativity of Declarative Networking. *Operating Systems Rev.*, 43(4):19–24, 2009. DOI: 10.1145/1713254.1713260 Cited on page(s) 87

Yun Mao, Boon Thau Loo, Zachary Ives, and Jonathan M. Smith. MOSAIC: Unified Platform for Dynamic Overlay Selection and Composition. In *Proc. Int. Conf. emerging Networking EXperiments and Technologies*, pages 1–12, 2008. DOI: 10.1145/1544012.1544017 Cited on page(s) 2, 3, 18, 87

William R. Marczak, David Zook, Wenchao Zhou, Molham Aref, and Boon Thau Loo. Declarative Reconfigurable Trust Management. In *Proc. 4th Biennial Conf. on Innovative Data Systems Research*, pages 1–9, 2009. Cited on page(s) 89, 92

William R. Marczak, Shan Shan Huang, Martin Bravenboer, Micah Sherr, Boon Thau Loo, and Molham Aref. SecureBlox: Customizable Secure Distributed Data Processing. In *Proc. ACM SIGMOD Int. Conf. on Management of Data*, pages 723–734, 2010. DOI: 10.1145/1807167.1807246 Cited on page(s) 18, 89, 92

MIT Chord. The Chord/DHash Project. `http://pdos.csail.mit.edu/chord/`. Cited on page(s) 71

David Mosberger and Larry L. Peterson. Making paths explicit in the Scout operating system. In *Proc. 2nd USENIX Symp. on Operating System Design and Implementation*, pages 153–167, 1996. DOI: 10.1145/238721.238771 Cited on page(s) 23

Shivkumar C. Muthukumar, Xiaozhou Li, Changbin Liu, Joseph B. Kopena, Mihai Oprea, Ricardo Correa, Boon Thau Loo, and Prithwish Basu. RapidMesh: declarative toolkit for rapid experimentation of wireless mesh networks. In *Proc. ACM Int. Workshop on Wireless Network Testbeds, Experimental Evaluation and Characterization*, pages 1–10, 2009a. DOI: 10.1145/1614293.1614295 Cited on page(s) 2, 25, 26, 87

Shivkumar C. Muthukumar, Xiaozhou Li, Changbin Liu, Joseph B. Kopena, Mihai Oprea, and Boon Thau Loo. Declarative toolkit for rapid network protocol simulation and experimentation. In *Proc. ACM Int. Conf. on Data Communication*, pages 1–2, 2009b. DOI: 10.1145/1614293.1614295 Cited on page(s) 2, 26

NetDB@Penn. http://netdb.cis.upenn.edu/. Cited on page(s) xv

Vivek Nigam, Limin Jia, Boon Thau Loo, and Andre Scedrov. Maintaining Distributed Logic Programs Incrementally. In *Proc. Int. ACM SIGPLAN Symp. on Principles and Practice of Declarative Programming*, pages 125–136, 2011. DOI: 10.1145/2003476.2003495 Cited on page(s) 40, 87

ns-3. Network Simulator 3. http://www.nsnam.org/. Cited on page(s) 2, 25

ORBIT. Wireless Network Testbed. http://www.orbit-lab.org/. Cited on page(s) 2, 25

M. Tamer Özsu and Patrick Valduriez. *Principles of Distributed Database Systems, Third Edition*. Prentice Hall, 2011. DOI: 10.1007/978-1-4419-8834-8 Cited on page(s) 2, 14

P2. Declarative Networking System. http://p2.cs.berkeley.edu/. Cited on page(s) xv, 5, 21, 55, 72, 82

Christopher R. Palmer, Phillip B. Gibbons, and Christos Faloutsos. ANF: A Fast and Scalable Tool for Data Mining in Massive Graphs. In *Proc. 8th ACM SIGKDD Int. Conf. on Knowledge Discovery and Data Mining*, pages 81–90, 2002. DOI: 10.1145/775047.775059 Cited on page(s) 81

Filip Perich. Policy-based Network Management for NeXt Generation Spectrum Access Control. In *Proc. IEEE Symp. on Dynamic Spectrum Access Networks*, pages 496–506, 2007. DOI: 10.1109/DYSPAN.2007.72 Cited on page(s) 96

Larry Peterson and Bruce Davie. *Computer Networks: A Systems Approach, Fourth Edition*. Morgan-KaufMann, 2007. Cited on page(s) 9, 10, 12, 49

PlanetLab. Global testbed. http://www.planet-lab.org/. Cited on page(s) 2

PVS. PVS Specification and Verification System. http://pvs.csl.sri.com/ (Accessed on Dec. 8, 2011). Cited on page(s) 89

Quagga. Routing Software Suite. http://www.quagga.net/. Cited on page(s) 95

Raghu Ramakrishnan and S. Sudarshan. Bottom-Up vs Top-Down Revisited. pages 321–336, 1999. Cited on page(s) 78

Raghu Ramakrishnan and Jeffrey D. Ullman. A Survey of Research on Deductive Database Systems. *J. Logic Programming*, 23(2):125–149, 1993. DOI: 10.1016/0743-1066(94)00039-9 Cited on page(s) 1, 7

Raghu Ramakrishnan, Kenneth A. Ross, Divesh Srivastava, and S. Sudarshan. Efficient Incremental Evaluation of Queries with Aggregation. In *Proc. ACM SIGMOD Int. Conf. on Management of Data*, pages 204–218, 1992. Cited on page(s) 36, 39

Venugopalan Ramasubramanian, Zygmunt J. Haas, and Emin Gun Sirer. SHARP: A Hybrid Adaptive Routing Protocol for Mobile Ad Hoc Networks. In *Proc. ACM Int. Symp. on Mobile Ad Hoc Networking and Computing*, pages 303–314, 2003. DOI: 10.1145/778415.778450 Cited on page(s) 82

RapidNet. RapidNet Declarative Networking Engine. `http://netdb.cis.upenn.edu/rapidnet/`. Cited on page(s) 2, 5, 25, 89

Yiqing Ren, Wenchao Zhou, Anduo Wang, Limin Jia, Alexander J.T. Gurney, Boon Thau Loo, and Jennifer Rexford. FSR: Formal Analysis and Implementation Toolkit for Safe Inter-domain Routing. In *Proc. ACM Int. Conf. on Data Communication*, pages 440–441, 2011. Cited on page(s) 89

Sean Rhea, Dennis Geels, Timothy Roscoe, and John Kubiatowicz. Handling Churn in a DHT. In *Proc. USENIX 2004 Annual Technical Conf.*, pages 10–10, 2004. Cited on page(s) 74, 75

J. Rohmer, R. Lescoeur, and J. M. Kerisit. Alexander Method - A Technique for the Processing of Recursive Axioms in Deductive Databases. *New Generation Computing*, 4(3):522–528, 1986. DOI: 10.1007/BF03037407 Cited on page(s) 78

S-BGP. Secure BGP. `http://www.ir.bbn.com/sbgp/`. DOI: 10.1109/DISCEX.2001.932219 Cited on page(s) 91

Domenico Saccà and Caro Zaniolo. Stable Models and Non-Determinism in Logic Programs with Negation. In *Proc. 9th ACM SIGACT-SIGMOD-SIGART Symp. on Principles of Database Systems*, pages 205–217, 1990. DOI: 10.1145/298514.298572 Cited on page(s) 88

Cesar Santivanez, Ram Ramanathan, and I. Stavrakakis. Making Link-state Routing Scale for Ad Hoc Networks. In *Proc. ACM Int. Symp. on Mobile Ad Hoc Networking and Computing*, pages 22–32, 2001. DOI: 10.1145/501416.501420 Cited on page(s) 27

Micah Sherr, Andrew Mao, William R. Marczak, Wenchao Zhou, Boon Thau Loo, and Matt Blaze. A3: An Extensible Platform for Application-Aware Anonymity. In *Proc. Network and Distributed Systems Security Symp.*, pages 1–20, 2010. Cited on page(s) 2, 89, 92

Atul Singh, Tathagata Das, Petros Maniatis, Peter Druschel, and Timothy Roscoe. BFT Protocols Under Fire. In *Proc. 5th USENIX Symp. on Networked Systems Design & Implementation*, pages 189–204, 2008. Cited on page(s) 2

Ion Stoica, Robert Morris, David Karger, M. Frans Kaashoek, and Hari Balakrishnan. Chord: A Scalable P2P Lookup Service for Internet Applications. In *Proc. ACM Int. Conf. on Data Communication*, pages 149–160, 2001. DOI: 10.1145/964723.383071 Cited on page(s) 59, 64, 74

Michael Stonebraker. Inclusion of New Types in Relational Data Base Systems. In *Proc. 2nd Int. Conf. on Data Engineering*, pages 262–269, 1986. Cited on page(s) 4, 52

S. Sudarshan and Raghu Ramakrishnan. Aggregation and Relevance in Deductive Databases. In *Proc. 17th Int. Conf. on Very Large Data Bases*, pages 501–511, 1991. Cited on page(s) 5, 77

D. Tennenhouse, J. Smith, W. Sincoskie, D. Wetherall, and G. Minden. A Survey of Active Network Research. *IEEE Commun. Mag.*, 35(1):80–86, 1997. DOI: 10.1109/35.568214 Cited on page(s) 4, 45

Amin Vahdat and David Becker. Epidemic Routing for Partially-Connected Ad Hoc Networks. Technical Report CS-200006, Durham, NC, 2000. Cited on page(s) 27

Arie van Deursen, Paul Klint, and Joost Visser. Domain-Specific Languages: An Annotated Bibliography. *ACM SIGPLAN Notices*, 35(6):26–36, 2000. DOI: 10.1145/352029.352035 Cited on page(s) 52

Laurent Vieille. Recursive Axioms in Deductive Database: The Query-Subquery Approach. In *Proc. 1st Int. Conf. on Expert Database Systems*, pages 253–267, 1986. Cited on page(s) 78

Anduo Wang, Prithwish Basu, Boon Thau Loo, and Oleg Sokolsky. Towards Declarative Network Verification. In *Proc. Int. Symp. on Practical Aspects of Declarative Languages*, pages 61–75, 2009. DOI: 10.1007/978-3-540-92995-6_5 Cited on page(s) 89

Anduo Wang, Limin Jia, Wenchao Zhou, Yiqing Ren, Boon Thau Loo, Jennifer Rexford, Vivek Nigam, Andre Scedrov, and Carolyn Talcott. FSR: Formal Analysis and Implementation Toolkit for Safe Inter-domain Routing. Technical Report MS-CIS-11-10, Philadelphia, PA, 2011. DOI: 10.1145/2018436.2018510 Cited on page(s) 88, 89

A. N. Wilschut and P. M. G. Apers. Pipelining in Query Execution. In *Proc. Int. Conf. on Databases, Parallel Architectures and their Applications*, pages 562–562, 1991. DOI: 10.1109/PARBSE.1990.77227 Cited on page(s) 24

Yices. An SMT Solver. http://yices.csl.sri.com/. Cited on page(s) 88

Wenchao Zhou, Eric Cronin, and Boon Thau Loo. Provenance-aware Secure Networks. In *Proc. Int. Conf. on Data Engineering Workshops*, pages 188–193, 2008. DOI: 10.1109/ICDEW.2008.4498315 Cited on page(s) 93

Wenchao Zhou, Yun Mao, Boon Thau Loo, and Martín Abadi. Unified Declarative Platform for Secure Networked Information Systems. In *Proc. 25th Int. Conf. on Data Engineering*, pages 150–161, 2009. DOI: 10.1109/ICDE.2009.58 Cited on page(s) 90, 91

Wenchao Zhou, Micah Sherr, Tao Tao, Xiaozhou Li, Boon Thau Loo, and Yun Mao. Efficient Querying and Maintenance of Network Provenance at Internet-Scale. In *Proc. ACM SIGMOD Int. Conf. on Management of Data*, pages 615–626, 2010. DOI: 10.1145/1807167.1807234 Cited on page(s) 93, 94

Wenchao Zhou, Ling Ding, Andreas Haeberlen, Zachary Ives, and Boon Thau Loo. TAP: Time-aware Provenance for Distributed Systems. In *Proc. USENIX Workshop on the Theory and Practice of Provenance*, pages 1–6, 2011a. Cited on page(s) 95

Wenchao Zhou, Qiong Fei, Arjun Narayan, Andreas Haeberlen, Boon Thau Loo, and Micah Sherr. Secure Network Provenance. In *Proc. 22nd ACM Symp. on Operating System Principles*, pages 295–310, 2011b. Cited on page(s) 93, 94, 95

Wenchao Zhou, Qiong Fei, Shengzhi Sun, Tao Tao, Andreas Haeberlen, Zachary Ives, Boon Thau Loo, and Micah Sherr. NetTrails: A Declarative Platform for Provenance Maintenance and Querying in Distributed Systems. In *Proc. ACM SIGMOD Int. Conf. on Management of Data*, pages 1323–1326, 2011c. DOI: 10.1145/1989323.1989488 Cited on page(s) 93, 94, 95

Authors' Biographies

BOON THAU LOO

Boon Thau Loo is an Assistant Professor in the Computer and Information Science department at the University of Pennsylvania. He received his Ph.D. degree in Computer Science from the University of California at Berkeley in 2006. Prior to his Ph.D., he received his M.S. degree from Stanford University in 2000, and his B.S. degree with highest honors from UC Berkeley in 1999. His research focuses on distributed data management systems, Internet-scale query processing, and the application of data-centric techniques and formal methods to the design, analysis and implementation of networked systems.

WENCHAO ZHOU

Wenchao Zhou is a Ph.D. student in the Computer and Information Science department at the University of Pennsylvania. He received his B.S. degree from Tsinghua University in 2006 and M.S. Degree from the University of Pennsylvania in 2009. His research interests are in distributed systems, focusing on logic-based declarative approach for verifiable secure distributed systems, and the application of data-centric techniques to secure forensics and diagnosis in potentially adversarial environments.